Alexis Denae Murphy

In

the

Closet

Finding Your Way Out When the Church Has Closed You In

DEDICATION

To the friend who shared her secret with me and to the friend who kept mine.

TABLE OF CONTENTS

CHAPTER I

No One Can Know

THERE I WAS, lying awake another restless night, nervously wondering how the relationship would end. It had been three months since my best friend told me she was in love with me, two months since I began to reciprocate those feelings, and one week since we crossed the line of no return. Both the wonders of love and the fear of loss kept my mind running endlessly until morning.

What keeps you up at night?

Is it the regret of something you've done?

Maybe it's the shock of being in the place you said you would never be.

If there was one situation I thought I would never find myself in, being romantically involved with a girl was at the top of my list. In my religious, 15-year-old mind, the Bible seemed clear on the lines of sexuality. I would have summed it up to the following:

Woman is made *from* and *for* men.

Sex is made *only for* marriage.

I was confined to those statements until my circumstances began to challenge them. Black-and-white thinking does not consider the gray space that many of us find ourselves living in. I have learned that the lines of love are blurry at best.

Attention can make the most insecure person grow in confidence. A hug can tear down a lifetime of walls built. A kiss can fulfill the longing of two souls. As a Christian, I longed for those precursors of love with a boy, yet I first experienced them with a girl. And though I tried my best to control who I loved, it was impossible to stop her from loving me.

Is that not an honest desire, to not only *give* love but to *receive* it? When love finds its way to us, what fool would turn it away? The package that love comes in hardly decreases the value of the gift. With time, even when tattered and torn, the package becomes as beautiful as the gift. Even though I was head over heels for her, my narrow theological scope led to great tension in my heart. There was a certain exhaustion that came only when trying to answer God-sized questions from a limited knowledge base. I would often ponder how God's love and goodness played into the situation and why He would allow this relationship to happen if same-sex relationships were wrong.

I never wanted to stay awake and figure out those questions alone. I wanted God to crack open the sky and speak to me as He did to Jesus at His baptism. I even prayed for flickering from the streetlights shining through my window—one flicker to end the relationship, two to stay in it. But I saw nothing. Silence, who was once my friend, became an enemy that only the sound of her voice could deafen. Thus, every night, we talked on the phone until I fell asleep.

If this had been a typical boy-girl relationship, a plethora of resources would have been available to help me sort my emotions. I would have had a community of people who understood me. I could not count how many times we discussed sex and relationships in my high school youth group at church. Though not necessarily wise advice, it came from experiences that bonded us together. We acknowledged that we were not perfect while doing our best to point each other to the One who is. Yet, in all my years of being in church, I had not heard one story of an attraction to the same sex. I wondered if this was *a common struggle for Christians or a sign I was not a Christian after all.*

I had exhausted all viable options from worldly sources. If I wanted answers about God and His thoughts on homosexuality, I figured the only place I could find them was from the church. My resolve did not bring the courage I needed for a conversation like this, but desperation did. During a midweek youth night, I hoped to boldly march into the church to confess all that I was dealing with but I could only muster up a slow walk crippled with fear.

I was on the verge of sharing my secret until someone in my youth group made a sharp remark about someone he knew. His words blazed like wildfire in a forest: "I just don't see how someone can be gay. It doesn't make sense." Like a tree, my body went aflame. Burning with shame, I remember very few details after that night. I withdrew into my inner shell that left me void of the small courage I once had. The church, the safest place I knew, quickly became a no-trespass zone. With yellow tape plastered over the doors that once welcomed me, I vowed to never tell my secret there.

More Than a Game

The unexpectancy of his words and insensitivity of his tone felt like a ball had been hurled at me full-speed and without warning, which is one reason I strongly dislike the game of dodgeball. The entire game is built on the premise of avoiding a black eye. At the beginning of the game, your speed to the half-court line determines whether you have the upper hand. If you reach the balls first, your team has the advantage. The caveat, however, is that if you are brave enough to sprint for the balls, you are at a greater risk of being hit. Likewise, if you are the last person standing, you are more vulnerable to getting hurt. It seems contradictory that to be a champion of dodgeball, you must embrace the risks that come with vulnerability. Yet, this dodgeball-like contradiction can be seamlessly paralleled with church hurt. As silly as it is to assume you will not be hit in dodgeball is the same as assuming you will not be offended in the church. Offense is inevitable.

Since sin came into the world, humanity has been broken. Our desires, motives, and actions have been tainted, causing even our best

3

intentions to fall short of the perfect goodness of God. Solomon says in Ecclesiastes 7:20 (NASB), "There is not a righteous man on earth who continually does good and who never sins." Solomon does not leave an exception for those who attend church, either. Sin is a fatal disease that has metastasized throughout all of humanity, including those who live within the body of Christ. Because of this, church hurt is prevalent, real, and worthy to be addressed.

One way church hurt manifests inside of people is through unmet expectations. The expectation for Christians is they *should* do all that Jesus *would* do, completely dismissing the key difference: No one has been able to and will ever be able to perfectly follow Jesus' example. Christ's call for His church is to be above reproach; however, the error in most people's thinking is that the church is solely responsible for meeting its congregants' expectations. People-pleasing has never been at the heart of God. His desire is for His children to be loved and this love can often be received as an uncomfortable, offensive feeling otherwise known as conviction. Don't get me wrong, that kid in my youth group was out of line and 110% needed a correction, but the hurt I was experiencing came from a place inside of me that shame had already claimed as its territory.

The deeper and more concerning issue with church hurt is that its victims project the action of God's people onto the attitude of God. Not everyone who leaves one congregation finds another; many times, they stop looking for God altogether. From the moment at that youth group meeting until one year later, I wanted nothing to do with the Bible, church, or God. If church people thought same-sex attraction was too much, how in the world did a holy God view me?

Maybe this is you as you recount the bruises that a church may have caused you. Have you felt the stares of disapproval as you walked into service with gender-opposite clothing? Have you needed prayer on an issue, but as you walked to the altar the number of head shakes and murmurs caused you to turn around? Has a Christian family member muttered a comment about another couple at Walmart yet completely in the dark about your sexual preferences? Worse, has a pastor or other leader flat out told you that you were not welcome there?

If the core of God's heart has always been to reunite with us, has church hurt caused more pain to God than His people? What if with every insensitive comment or discriminatory remark, one person were to walk away from faith? What happens when the very people a church prays that God saves are the same people they condemn to hell? How will change happen when we cancel our prayers with our bias?

Whether these gestures have been intentional or careless, the damage has been done. People live with insecurities caused by someone else's insensitivity. God's plan to reconcile His relationship with a fallen people has always been Jesus. Souls are set free when our desire for salvation is dressed in the sensitivity of Christ.

Closed In

It has been six years since I ended that high-school relationship, yet the remnants of the shame I felt that night at youth group lingered into my college years. I called off our relationship at the beginning of my senior year of high school because it was becoming physically and emotionally unhealthy. We became possessive and completely isolated ourselves from our former community. We were driven by however we felt in the moment. I did not walk away from her for holy reasons, but there was a holy pursuit happening in the midst.

Allow me to shine a moment of light into your present darkness: It may seem like you are going from one toxic relationship to another, but it is really God pursuing a personal relationship with you. The dissatisfaction from your partner is leading you to find fulfillment elsewhere. When physical bandages are taped over emotional abuse, it is only a matter of time until your need for healing is exposed again. Yelling over each other brings attention to your deep longing to be heard. Your constant efforts to please her are only a reflection of the amount of pleasure you are lacking.

Are you beginning to notice that the void of your heart is too big, too wide, and too deep for any earthly person to fill, and that external outbursts are only a minuscule expression of your inner turmoil? If that is true, would you be open to the possibility that God might not view you as other people have viewed you in the past?

If you are moments away from closing this book forever, let me just say this: I understand. Adjusting the lens of your perspective to the light of truth can be torturous and unbearable. There is a reason you feel stuck between needing to leave and wanting to stay. The motivation to hide is the same grounds for wanting to be free—solitude is scary.

There is a story in John 8 of a woman who had not one but several relationships at a time. I can only infer by experience that her dissatisfaction in one relationship led her to seek satisfaction in another. Regardless, at the loneliest time in her life, Jesus changed her story and set her free.

> Early in the morning, he came again to the temple. All the people came to him, and he sat down and taught them. The scribes and the Pharisees brought a woman who had been caught in adultery, and placing her in the midst they said to him, "Teacher, this woman has been caught in the act of adultery. Now in the Law, Moses commanded us to stone such women. So what do you say?" This they said to test him, that they might have some charges to bring against him. Jesus bent down and wrote with his finger on the ground. And as they continued to ask him, he stood up and said to them, "Let him who is without sin among you be the first to throw a stone at her." And once more he bent down and wrote on the ground. But when they heard it, they went away one by one, beginning with the older ones, and Jesus was left alone with the woman standing before him. Jesus stood up and said to her, "Woman, where are they? Has no one condemned you?" She said, "No one, Lord." And Jesus said, "Neither do I condemn you; go, and from now on sin no more" (John 8:2-11 ESV).

This unnamed woman was caught naked in the middle of a scandalous affair. As if the act itself was not embarrassing enough, she was caught by the most religious authorities at the time. I imagine she pleaded for them to let her be. Instead, they dragged her into a holy temple, interrupting a lesson taught by a well-known teacher at that time. Thrown into a pit of men and completely uncovered, she stood defenselessly awaiting her conviction to be killed. Not even shame could compete with how degraded she must have felt. Just moments prior, she was content on the sidelines of another person's marriage, yet she quite literally became the center of attention. The religious scribes and Pharisees did not cower from the opportunity to break the silence of this awkward moment by pointing out her sin and then suggesting her punishment.

The scribes were scholars of the Old Testament Law, also known as the Mosaic Law, which is the Law of Moses. The Pharisees were a group that relied heavily on the Law while strongly believing sinners deserved death. Both of these authorities came together often to trap Jesus so they would have grounds to kill Him. We will later discuss Jesus more in-depth, but for now, it is enough to know that He also knew the Law. As students of the Mosaic Law, the religious authorities knew an adulterous act was grounds for death (Lev. 20:10). Scripture says their motive was not only aimed at destroying the woman's image, but they also wanted to ruin Jesus' reputation.

Even though this story happened millennia ago, it sounds familiar. I always cringe when I hear some people recall scripture. I realized it is not the words themselves but the motivation behind them. For the scribes and Pharisees, quoting scripture was not for salvanic purposes. It was quite the opposite. They aimed to prove why she should not be saved. The scribes and Pharisees were convinced that this woman's sin deserved death, and if Jesus disagreed, He should be killed, too.

I ache for her back then, and I ache for us today.

There are Christians among us today who want sinners condemned more than saved. If the first scripture that comes to mind when you see two men holding hands is "the wages of sin is death," then you have a problem similar to the Pharisees that needs to be addressed. Too often do one of our hands hold the mallet while the other holds the stone when we were never given the authority to judge or condemn others. Be that as it may, the religious authorities did one thing right—they brought her to Jesus.

They did not know that in bringing her broken soul to Jesus, He was already waiting. Jesus' first action was nothing like the crowd's. His first motion was to bend down. At this rock-bottom moment in her life, the true Rock floated beneath her feet to steady her. Relief met her for a moment as all eyes shifted from her to Him for the first time since she arrived.

He began to write a message while the crowd demanded an answer for her fate. Breaking His focus, He stood and gave permission to stone her under one condition. The only one who could kill her must be found *without sin*. As the story continues, the commotion dies down as the crowd files out of the temple. Yes, even the scribes and Pharisees. As mentioned before, Jesus not only knew the Law, but He kept it perfectly. Ironic that the condition of her death could only be met by Him. Yet, He chose to humble Himself and spare her life. Jesus bent down again and did not stand up until every person left. After the room was clear, Jesus stood and called her to sin no more.

The Breaking Point

For several years now, I've had the privilege of doing outreach with high school kids after school. I love that they are bold and bendable at the same time. It is the perfect age to enjoy them as kids while empowering them to become the best versions of themselves as young adults.

Our ministry welcomes every kid whether they are interested in what we preach. Of course, we would love for professions of faith to happen after all of our hangouts, but we know that the Holy Spirit moves in His time. We are simply called to be faithful stewards of what and who He has given us.

I had one special friend that I will call Nora (for confidentiality purposes). Our organization had privileges to school lunches which allowed us to meet several new students at a time. I did not actually meet Nora at lunch, but I noticed that she sat at the same table each time I visited. She was full of energy, always smiling and cracking jokes. Not only was she a stellar student but a highly skilled basketball player, too. Side note: I also played basketball in high school which was my go-to affinity group in ministry.

I never personally invited her to our weekly meeting, though she happened to show up with a group of friends one Monday night. Again, Nora was the life of the party, sometimes too lively as I often sent soft glares to her during our short leader sermons at the end of the night.

Week after week, Nora would consistently show up. Over time, I began to notice a slight difference in her interactions with one of her friends in the group. They possessed a certain closeness that reminded me of my friendship in high school. Unfortunately, when they were together, it became nearly impossible to engage in a five-minute conversation with either of them. They seemed to need each other... for everything.

Eventually, Nora and her friend stopped coming to our meetings. I learned they had been dating and were recently broken up. After this, the only times I saw her were at her basketball games, in which I noticed the fun and bubbly girl that lit up every room had succumbed to darkness. Teachers, family, and her friends had given up on her. She was only seen as delinquent and "too far gone."

About a year later, I was allowed the privilege of doing devotionals with the girls' basketball team before practice. I would prepare a team-building game, bring snacks, and open the Bible to share a brief lesson. One evening, Nora came in mid-discussion, threw herself in a chair, and hysterically cried with her head down on the desk. I realized the already little attention I had from the other girls disappeared as Nora came in, so I dismissed them for practice.

I knew this was the moment to press in, but I had not exchanged more than a few words with her over the past year. The silence was deafening but it was crucial that I said something, and unlike the Pharisees, I wanted to be loving and a listener.

I walked to the desk in front of her, sat down, and asked softly, "Do you want to talk about it?"

Like an episode of intractable vomiting, her words spilled uncontrollably from her mouth. Not everything she said was whole, though. Most of her sentences were fragmented in bits and pieces in between heavy breaths and tears. She mentioned a little about falling in love and being betrayed, getting into trouble and disobeying her mom, and feeling alone, lost, and unclean. The words I remember are shared below, as she unknowingly spoke for a multitude of people going through the same thing.

Nora said, "I know you love God, but I don't think He can love me. My parents are religious and have told me that being gay is wrong. I used to be so close with my mom, and now, we argue all of the time. I can't help how I feel. She just doesn't understand. Ever since my ex-girlfriend walked into my life, I don't know who I am or where I'm going. I'm so lost."

Nora was fully aware that her soul was lost. She felt alone and abandoned like the woman in the Bible. The hiding and pretending were too exhausting to continue. She had reached her breaking point. At rock bottom, she was desperate for a savior. I prayed with her that night, and I want to offer you the same prayer:

Dear God,

I come to You at this moment, not only for myself but also on behalf of my precious readers. Their souls have been shattered and torn. Feelings of hopelessness and abandonment cloud their vision. Help them to see that You succeed where others have failed. Your love surpasses the love this world can offer. Father, You know they feel lost, but we know Your Word says that no one will snatch us from Your hands. You allow the 99 to file out, so You can focus on the one—the one who has exhausted all other options, the one who is helpless and exposed, and the one who longs for deep healing. Will You soften their hearts to begin to receive Jesus as the answer? Grant them peace of mind at night to rest in the hope that their solitude is part of Your redemptive plan. Allow them to see that there is no sinner whom Jesus is unwilling to save.

In Jesus' name, Amen.

We do not know the message Jesus wrote in the dirt to the adulterous woman, but His message to me at the peak of my shame was, "My grace is sufficient for you." As we journey toward freedom, we will begin to unravel the mystery of this all-sufficient grace. Jesus has proven enough for me, friend. He can be enough for you, too.

CHAPTER II

Hide-n-Seek

I HAVE FOUND THAT the worst part of a dying relationship is how long its memories continue to live. As if the breakup itself isn't hard enough, we then go through the agonizing process to rid ourselves of tangible sentiments from the other person. The gifts that once brought the heart a happy flutter now trigger a painful throb. Not to mention, a pinch of guilt creeps in as the snapshots of good memories fool us into neglecting the reality of the bad ones.

For the remainder of my senior year, post-breakup, I was a single and anxious wreck. I only found relief when my mind was occupied with school or basketball. I thought if I could make it through the next five months, I would be free of the tortuous past of high school and finally start over in college. I did not know that surviving the present would entail a future of barely surviving each second of every day.

Each time I would see her in the halls or recognize a car like hers, the thoughts of all that we shared began to haunt me. There was one day in particular that I was driving to a store to run an errand, and a memory of ours danced through the center of my thoughts. In attempting to control the thought, I lost control of my steering wheel. I'm thankful the other car adjusted quickly to avoid what would have been a head-on collision. I then found the nearest lot and parked my car.

That day, I was fortunate to avoid physical, life-threatening injuries and irreparable damage to my car, but my mental and spiritual state was not so lucky. I was in total disbelief that my simple, teenage life had become full of fear and anxiety. I was fearful that my reputation was at stake. If I were to share all that happened in my relationship over the past 11 months, I would no longer be seen as the good Christian girl with a bright future ahead nor would I blend in with the non-problematic kids. I would be the newest topic of gossip among family and friends bringing disgrace to my parents and church members. The thought of this brought about more anxiety of the possibility of being more alone.

I was ashamed of not only who I had become but who I may have always been. Maybe I didn't stumble into the relationship after all. What if I was already predestined to same-sex attraction and this was my life now?

Cozy Condemnation

What is shame?

Is it more than regret?

Is it the same as guilt?

How does it manifest in our lives?

It is imperative to know *what* shame is before we know *how* to diminish its power.

Shame is a painful feeling of humiliation or distress caused by the consciousness of wrong or foolish behavior. From Oxford's definition, we can understand the meaning of shame in three parts. Shame is a *feeling* caused by *the consciousness* of wrong *behavior.*[1]

The feeling of shame is what *leads* us to our closet.

The consciousness of shame is what *confines* us in our closet.

The wrong behavior that initiates shame is what *returns* us to our closet.

Most of us can readily identify with the feeling of shame. This is usually a season of life characterized by regret, resentment, and loneliness when we walk away from our community with others. Thus, the danger of feeling ashamed is that our voices are the only ones we permit to speak back to us. We go into hiding by not allowing others the opportunity to respond to what caused our shame in the first place. In other words, we strip the crowd from the chance to humiliate us by shaming ourselves first.

The consciousness of shame is less identifiable as it has everything to do with our relationship with Christ or lack thereof. Scripture says, "Even Gentiles, who do not have God's written law, show that they know his law then they instinctively obey it... for their conscience and thoughts either accuse them or tell them they are doing right" (Rom. 2:14-15 NLT). This means that even those who do not acknowledge God for who He is knows the difference between right and wrong. Our consciousness bears witness to absolute truth. That is, it confirms that an absolute God exists.

Still, our consciousness holds little weight toward our actions. We must remember that once sin entered the world, all that was good became broken. Just because one has a strong feeling or belief that something is right or wrong, it can only be approved by correctly handling the truth, which is God's Word.[2]

At a time when I severely doubted my faith, a sliver of light shined beneath my closet door once I considered why I chose to hide. Not even a tarnished reputation would have kept me in such a dark and lonely place. In 2 Corinthians 4:2 (NRSV), Paul says, "We have renounced the shameful things that one hides" implying that those who see their actions as shameful will hide. Titus 1:15 (ESV) similarly says, "To the pure, all things are pure, but to the defiled and unbelieving, nothing is pure; but both their minds and their consciences are defiled."

Once you begin to recognize that you are confined by your actions *because* you consider them worthy of shame, I pray you receive the same glimpse of hope given to me. We must remember not everyone with same-sex desires keeps them a secret. Your desire to be pure attests to a work happening in you and not of you. The only path to a renewed conscience is by the washing of Christ's blood over us. If Paul, a true Christian, and the rest of the Church have renounced these behaviors through Jesus Christ, you can, too. It is very possible that your unclear conscience is a sign of hope that God is, indeed, pursuing a relationship with you.

Lastly, the wrong behavior that initiates shame is what causes us to return to our closet. Our best intentions can lead to the worst results. I cannot recount the number of times I told myself I was done, that I would not call her, text her, or meet up. Or, if we did meet up, I told myself that we would not argue, fight or engage in sexual activity. Nonetheless, my willpower proved insufficient during those moments of weakness. After repeated mistakes, I began to believe the closet is where I deserved to be.

How often do you relate to Paul when he said, "For I do not what I want, but I do the very thing I hate" (Rom. 7:15 ESV)? The inner storm of lust is often too turbulent to quiet on our own. Human willpower is unable to resist such a vicious force of nature. And so, when our good intentions fail us time and time again, we put on a cloak of shame once more.

You see, shame is like a weighted blanket of self-hate that keeps us cozy and condemned in our closet. When we begin to blend the disappointment of what we have done with the displeasure of who we are, our souls become deeply vulnerable. We become unable to give or receive love from other people, and due to the way we despise ourselves, the need to "be different" begins to erupt.

Self-hate rears its ugly head in many forms, and sexuality is at the top of that list. Many people who have opted to change their identity or become another gender altogether thought at some point that they were created wrong. I have heard some of my friends say, "I was meant to be a..." as if the Creator of the Universe made a fundamental error in forming them. Sometimes it is societal norms they do not fit into, whether a male enjoying cheerleading or a female with broader shoulders. Even worse, bullies called them "gay" or a "tomboy" until those labels began to become part of how they saw themselves.

Dear reader, I know this is a hard place to meddle, but it is important to know the root cause of your actions. For far too long, you have blamed your fluid identity on low self-esteem and insecurities when it is actually shame manifesting full force in your life. Each of us has a deep desire to be covered and we long to feel safe. However, the blanket of shame is only a cheap version of what we truly seek. God's presence is what we lack. Though we wish to be discovered on our terms, He has a longstanding record of finding what is hidden.

No Wiggle Room

Imagine being the first human to ever live. You are the embodiment of a perfect stature and a flawless complexion. There is no stress about losing weight or tanning beds because you are the prototype of humanity. As you prance through Eden's garden, you see various species that differentiate them from you. Your appreciation of all that is unique allows your soul to soar with the birds that *you* named. When you pass a body of water, you see your reflection as a work of art. Freedom and joy flow simultaneously through your bones as you are content with simply being. You have found pure satisfaction in living without want when God forms a perfect companion from your bones. Solitude was enough, yet company was given out of abundance. The Creator gave each of you two names to distinguish the human species: man and woman. For the first time, you are able to admire someone else made in the same likeness as you. She resembles grace, resilience, and beauty. All the needs you never knew you had are finally met.

Like the first humans, Adam and Eve lived this unfathomable reality. They knew exactly what it meant to exceed in appreciation, joy, and contentment. Genesis 2:25 (ESV) says they "were both naked and were not ashamed." Provided that this is not our current reality, as we are clothed humans locked away by the effects of shame, what happened? When did it all change?

Just before Eve was created, God gave Adam instructions on maintaining the Earth. Genesis 2:15-17 (ESV) reads:

> The Lord God took the man and put him in the garden of Eden to work it and keep it. And the Lord God commanded the man, saying, "You may surely eat of every tree of the garden, but of the tree of the knowledge of good and evil you shall not eat, for in the day that you eat of it you shall surely die."

We will see in the following chapter what happens when God's words are distorted, but we must first lay them out to dissect. The commandment God gave Adam consisted of a *do* and a *don't*.

Do eat of every tree in the garden.

Don't eat of the tree of the knowledge of good and evil.

Often, as I have read this scripture or heard it talked about, the *do* portion is forgotten. It seems easier to focus on what Adam could not do than what he actually had permission to do. God gave Adam the authority to eat from every tree. I mean, the garden was practically an endless buffet of fruit, vegetables, and meat. His options were limitless, and we would assume he had more than enough to enjoy but apparently not since he eventually ate from the prohibited tree.

Due to this, I have judged Adam on many occasions, but how can I judge him when I am similar? It takes no effort for me to complain about what I do not have while completely forgetting all that I do have. When my plate is full, I want to cram on more. Worse, sometimes, I want to throw the whole gourmet dish away to grab cheap fast food instead. How absurd that I would rather spend money to get a cheap and less healthy meal than to enjoy the higher quality meal already provided for me at home? The point I am making is that our desire for more is insatiable, and it started at the beginning of time.

Many people think if God gave them more wiggle room, then they would not have to be rebellious. Unfortunately, that is not how sin works. When your heart is turned away from God, you walk further from Him regardless of what He offers you because your gaze is focused elsewhere.

It is not until you turn back to Him that your rebellion starts to fade. Just as a good God created a perfect world and sculpted perfect humans to inhabit it, He also had a perfect plan for each of our lives.

The limitations in the realm of sexuality are tighter to maneuver since more is at stake. Scripture clearly states that sex is *only* permissible within the boundaries of marriage. This is not a debatable topic. 1 Corinthians 7:2 (ESV) reads, "But because of the temptation to sexual immorality, each man should have his own wife and each woman her own husband." Just as the line was clearly drawn for Adam in what he should eat, it is as evident that sex is to be shared only between a husband and wife.

God has given us a *do* and a *don't* regarding sexual relations. Along with His commandment, there is a consequence associated. *Do* have sex within the boundaries of marriage. *Don't* have sex outside of marriage. If you *do* what I tell you not to do, then the consequence is death. Hence, shame is the byproduct of disobedience while death is the ultimate punishment for living outside of the boundaries of God. We see the first account of shame in humanity in Genesis 3:8 (ESV). It reads:

> And they heard the sound of the Lord God walking in the garden in the cool of the day, and the man and his wife hid from the presence of the Lord God among the trees of the garden.

The story picks up immediately after Adam and Eve ate from the tree. Before their disobedience, God's presence kindled joy and delight. Both Adam and Eve were unafraid, living in the bliss of contentment. Being that God is omnipresent, meaning His presence is everywhere, it is safe to conclude that Adam and Eve were in perfect and harmonious unity with Him. Though when they neglected to follow God's instruction, their union with God was broken. Even still, the separation itself does not give meaning to their act of hiding. The simple solution to separation is to be reunited. Running away from His presence seems counterintuitive since this was their Creator. So, what caused Adam and Eve to hide? What invoked fear and shame?

If God Were Good

In my freshman year of high school, I was on an all-star basketball team. Each night, we would alternate our starting five. We were that stacked with exceptional talent and skill. Granted, I never played a varsity game that whole season. My teammate and I sat at the end of the bench, faithfully taking stats each night. Surprisingly, as competitive as I was, it did not bother me not to accrue any playing time that year. I was proud to wear the same jersey, grab water bottles during timeouts, and catch rebounds for the upperclassmen. I was satisfied to simply be a part of the team.

We were undefeated during our regulation season, scoring over 60 points a game. The local news would show up to our home games, which was a big deal, given boys' basketball teams were usually the only ones receiving that type of coverage. Word spread around town, and eventually, no one wanted to play us. Being a part of an all-star team brought feelings of pride and joy whereas being on the opposing team brought them feelings of fear and intimidation. Perspective made all the difference in how we chose to approach each other.

With this in mind, we go back to Adam and Eve's inclination to hide. When they were connected with God, or on His team, they lived in dignity with Him and had high self-esteem. It was not an ungodly pride but more so confidence of knowing who and whose they were. However, when they sinned, the separation put them at odds with God or on the opposing team, if you will. Even though they *knew* God, sin caused them to forget His goodness and their identity.

The limits that God gave Adam and Eve were good like the limits He gives us. Because sin has entered the world and equally lives inside of us, we doubt His good intentions and stop believing He knows best. Our perception of God demotes Him to be the bad guy as we lift ourselves above Him to be the new creator of the law.

We act as if God's legislation can be changed based on popular opinions and mere feelings. I am aware there are millions of people within the LGBTIQA+ community with rainbow flags in their bios and a faithful attendance to pride marches. I realize there are laws now and, in the making, to give this group more political rights. There is a process by which our man-made systems follow to bring about change. However, we must not neglect what God has already ordained as unchanging.

As hard as it is to accept, God's boundaries and His limits are good, especially in the realm of sexuality. His laws are perfect, firm, and unwavering. Trust me when I say I have wrestled with this tension long and hard. Just as Adam may have thought *why not that tree,* I have also asked God *why sex only in a heterosexual marriage? Why only with a man?* The answer is simply because He said so. I have desired the other trees in the garden of sex that were off-limits. I have actually eaten from them, and it has only brought further separation that eventually led to a hardness of heart toward God.

A hard heart is untrusting of God's goodness. Doubt freezes over your desire to do His Will. The heart becomes like an immovable brick, dragging you down to the ocean floor of your ways. Like a boulder that cannot be penetrated, no one can shift your thinking. Joined with darkness, you begin to drift away from anyone or anything that disagrees with your set course of action.

You may not even recognize that your heart has begun to stiffen toward the goodness of God. Here is a short list of indicators to help gauge the spiritual rigidity of your heart:

- If God were good, He would not allow me to have same-sex desires.
- If God were good, He would let me and my significant other be happy.
- If God were good, He would have stopped me from being abused as a child.
- If God were good, I would have more attention from the opposite sex.

- If God were good, life would not be this hard.
- If God were good, I would have a community to open up to that would not judge me.

The cry of your heart is aching for a good God to prove His goodness to you. The desires of your heart, the trauma from your past, and the life you want to live demand intervention from God, and that is exactly what He desires to do: intervene.

Where Are You?

"But the Lord God called to the man and said to him, 'Where are you?' And he said, 'I heard the sound of you in the garden, and I was afraid, because I was naked, and I hid myself.'"
(GENESIS 3:9-10 ESV)

In these short verses, we observe the first account of the familiar game we know as Hide-n-Seek. Frankly, it seems silly for Adam and Eve to participate in such a game with the all-knowing, all-present God, but we must remember that separation from God through their disobedience caused their perspective of God to faultily shift. Also, recall that Adam and Eve "were naked and unashamed" before they sinned. Only after walking outside of the boundaries of God did their eyes open to their nakedness. Then, they sewed fig leaves to cover themselves.[3]

It is common to mistake their original nakedness as a lack of protection as a reason for them to seek shelter, but this is not true. The need for covering has always been in the makeup of humanity. The absence of this is only the aftermath of their failure to obey. God's presence filled the garden upon the creation of the world. Humanity's new realization of their condition after sin further proves that separation from God, in fact, clouds the minds of those who disobey. Therefore, we can conclude that before sin, God's presence was sufficient in protecting and covering them.

Furthermore, we see that sin not only changes our perspective of God but also has the power to reshape our posture toward Him. Before the fall, humanity had a posture that symbolized an open and intimate relationship with each other and with God. There was no fear of judgment, need for clothes, or desire to compare. They possessed a perfect vertical-horizontal balance in that God's presence dwelled around them and within them, allowing an overflow of Him to be poured into each other.

After Adam and Eve disobeyed God, their posture went from open to closed off. Crouched behind a bush, they did not want to be found. They were no longer naked but clothed with leaves of shame. And still, they perceived themselves as exposed causing them to hunker down and cower away from God. Notice how gracious God was not to impose as He could have easily ambushed their hiding place. Instead, scripture says the Lord God called out to the man and extended the invitation for them to identify their location.

Make no mistake—Your act of sin, the choice to hide, and the hardness of your heart are not exemptions from Hide-n-Seek but qualifications to participate in the story of The Great Reconciliation. God pursues you in the same way He pursued Adam and Eve. Even after you choose the opposite of His Will for your life, He seeks after you. He desires to be with you and restore your broken union.

The greatest act of deception from Satan is for you to believe that shame is about the apple when it is really about abandoning the Creator of the tree. The tree of sexual promiscuity has a variety of choices. There's the apple of homosexuality, the apple of promiscuity, and the apple of bisexuality. There is an option to be transgender or pansexual; genderqueer or gender fluid; and asexual or self-pleasing. Again, the apples are only distractions to the bigger issue.

Viewing both sides of the open and close-minded debate, God is the perfect portion to balance the scale. He opened His mind to create every detail of the world as we know it. He was not narrow in His thinking when He made the seas, the land, and the stars. As the true Artist, He meticulously introduced the concept of our senses while offering assortments tailored to each creature. God was and has always been the definition of freedom, as scripture says, "Now the Lord is the Spirit, and where the Spirit of the Lord is, there is freedom" (2 Cor. 3:17 ESV). It is only our finite minds that belittle His craftsmanship to consider Him crass.

Identical to his openness, God also closed the discussion for debate by forming limits, boundaries, and rules for His inhabitants to remain safe. Our freedom lies within His Will. A discussion to improvise what God has already cast provision for is comical at best. We cannot rise above the Creator and make demands. There is no winning any debate on God's Word, and quite frankly, God has never been the type to argue. Thus, the case of open-mindedness versus closed-mindedness to justify or invalidate a lifestyle in favor of or opposition to God's law is a dead end. It is simple: to obey God's commands is to choose freedom, and to disobey God's commands is to choose death.

God's question stands: "Where are you?" But I find a better question to ask first: *Do you know where you are?*

Your physical location is important, but also consider your emotional, mental, and spiritual state of being. *Where has shame taken you?* The golden rule in fixing any problem is to first acknowledge your part in it. Below I have crafted a list of questions for you to process. Take some time to journal through these questions before continuing to the next chapter. Regardless of where your answers fall, I want to challenge you to denounce your shame and uncover yourself to a God who I have experienced to be good. He will bring clarity to your clouded vision and freedom to the life He has breathed into you.

Physical: Where do you spend the majority of your time and with who? Are you currently involved in a romantic relationship? How much time do you spend together? How often are you alone? Do you include your partner in your alone time? When you do something you are not proud of, where is the first place you go? Do you have anywhere to go? What is your comfort food? Do you indulge often? Do you live an active or inactive lifestyle? Does your activity change depending on your relationship status?

Emotional: How do you feel right now? How do you define feeling good? When are you happiest? Who brings about that happiness? How often do you prioritize your happiness? Do you protect it? When are you saddest? What makes you proud? What causes you to feel defeated? Do you struggle with anxiety? Do you find yourself depressed and unmotivated?

Mental: What are you thinking right now? On what basis do you ground yourself (i.e., philosophies, religions, etc.)? How many of your decisions are based on what other people think? Whose voice do you hear when you make important decisions? When you do something you are not proud of, whose face comes to mind? Are you a deep thinker? Would you rather "turn it off" by engaging in other activities? Do you trust the voice in your head?

Spiritual: Were you raised in the church? Do you consider yourself a spiritual person? Do you believe there is a God? If so, has your god been good to you? Do you believe there are multiple gods? If heaven is real, how does one get in? What about hell? What is your current view of the church? Are you hardened toward the church? Does your picture of church resemble your image of God? Do you believe someone can be a Christian while living how they want?

CHAPTER III

Fooled Me Once

WOULD YOU SAY that you strive to be a good person? Most people do. While some will easily admit to having made poor decisions, they would also argue that those decisions were justified by good intentions. Not many of us wake up and say, "How can I be worse of a person today?" or, "I think I will lessen the quality of my life and the lives of those around me." The Branch family is a prime example of how choices rooted in good intentions often leave unwanted results.

Joe Branch was a man that lived in the metropolitan area of Savannah, Georgia. He met his wife in college at Georgia Tech and resided there once they graduated. Upon having their second child, Joe lost his job and began to search for another as his wife, Tara, stayed at home and schooled their oldest daughter. Months had gone by with no luck for them. Consequently, Joe began an irreversible habit of stopping by the bar for a drink on the way home from his job-hunting endeavors. One drink led to two until he found himself with no family as Tara took their children to move back with her parents in Ohio.

I guarantee that Joe and Tara did not plan on becoming alcoholics or single parents when dreaming of their future as a family. They were college graduates, had stable incomes, and, for the most part, lived a simple life. Now that Joe and Tara are divorced, who is to blame? Was

Joe justified in his drinking problem due to his struggle to cope with unemployment? Did Tara have proper reasons to leave him, or was she to fight harder for their marriage? Who was more wrong in this situation? Moreover, who is to blame for how their children are affected by the separation? As innocent as their intentions may have been, the choices made had life-altering consequences.

Similarly, Adam and Eve did not intend to be disobedient to God in the garden of Eden, but they were. Eve ate the fruit from the tree and then convinced Adam to do the same. Was Eve to blame since she ate from the tree first, or was Adam at fault for not refusing her offer? We dove into the act of disobedience in the last chapter, but we will now focus on what causes disobedience and who is actually at fault for sin. My hope is that you will better understand what it is that leads us into unwanted situations despite our good intentions, and how our honest efforts often produce undesirable outcomes.

Timeless War

> "What has been will be again, what has been done will be done
> again; there is nothing new under the sun."
> (ECCLESIASTES 1:9 NIV)

What if you knew you were not a lone ranger in the battle of same-sex attraction? The first time I had heard of someone "struggling" with homosexuality as a Christian was at a basketball camp in Georgia. I had just graduated high school and decided to serve the camp as a counselor. On the last day of training before the campers arrived, one of our leaders shared her testimony. I had known of her name for the past four years, but not her story. She began by saying that this moment was not for her, but for someone else in the room.

Chills ran down my spine and my muscles began to quiver. I am surprised to this day that no one has asked me if I was epileptic or prone to panic attacks. Honestly, anytime anyone shares anything personal about themselves, my stomach takes a special interest in gymnastics and I cannot sit still. But I digress.

The speaker's story began a lot like mine. She was roommates with a girl, who eventually became a close friend. As time went on, they became more affectionate toward one another but not in a platonic way. Eventually, a moment arose between them and they had their first kiss. She was shocked by this because she was not attracted to her friend, or not that she knew of. Her story ended with them no longer being roommates or friends. God came into her life and revealed that it was Him she was missing. He embraced her in the middle of the night, and she has been living for Him ever since.

I was minutes away from losing my marbles. Her testimony was so triggering that it took supernatural restraint not to hyperventilate in my chair. As if it wasn't enough that she just read my whole life, she then encouraged each of us to partner with a stranger and share our last five percent.

Excuse me?

I took offense to this challenge because although she was courageous enough to uncover her skeletons, I was just fine keeping mine underneath my skin. After all, I did not come to this camp for me but to share Christ with a team of high school girls. How did this become about the leaders?

Despite my opposition, a girl by the name of Kate claimed me as her partner. We were walking to an isolated place, and my mind was racing to think of something so secretive that was the furthest from my actual truth. Do you ever do that? Slowly peel back layers so that someone can feel like they really know you, and they still have no clue? I thought of something to avoid being vulnerable, but I can't remember it now. I only remember Kate asking me, "Do you want to go first?" I said, "Yes." Then, told her every detail of my high school love story.

It felt less like talking and more like the vomitous spill that my friend Nora had done to me. Quite literally, there was something rotten inside of me that needed to be removed immediately. I had pushed it down one time too many, and poor Kate bore the brunt of it all. I had just met this girl and could not help but release all of the hurt, grief, and confusion I had been suppressing over the past year. I expected her to get up a couple of sentences in, but she never moved. I saw no looks of disgust either. She sat there, locked in, with an occasional "mhm" and "wow." Once I finished, I looked straight ahead, still trembling from my heightened anxiety. I had been running from that moment of judgment for over a year since that one night at Bible study. I braced myself for whatever harsh words were coming.

God could not have created a better person for me to out my secret to because Kate did not react how I anticipated. She simply looked at me with watery eyes and said, "You are so brave for sharing your life with me. Your story will change so many lives." Little did she know, she changed my life at that moment. It was the first time in over a year that I felt lighter, stronger, and a little less disgusting than I thought I was. Kate's compassionate words silenced all of the thoughts telling me that I would be hated, ostracized, and judged. She embraced my vomit so I could embrace the peace of God. The brave soul who shared the last parts of herself with a room full of strangers motivated me to do the same. Even though I wanted to tuck my secret away, the light of Jesus in Kate provided safety for me to be liberated, too.

I wish courageous moments like those superseded the times of despair I have faced. Seeing a lineage of people fight similar battles has taken me through bouts of hopefulness and depression. While it is comforting to know that I am not an anomaly, it can be quite discouraging to know that sexual fluidity and the crisis of identity are timeless wars.

One of the earliest accounts of same-sex attraction is found in Greek history. Though they did not use contemporary terms like "homosexuality" or "lesbian," it is indeed seen across their regions and among their theatrics. Unlike Western culture, the grounds for such an attraction were based on preference rather than moralistic views. Ancient

Rome was among the first to demoralize homosexuality even before Christianity became influential.[4]

Believe it or not, no one has ever woken up from their sleep with an intense desire for their friend. Same-sex relationships are more than attraction and passion bubbling over for another person but a slow burn that has been brewing since the beginning of time. There is a method to and a mastermind behind the madness. You no longer have to settle in ignorance nor must you accept the defeat of waging a war with yourself when Satan is the culprit scheming behind the scenes. He is the one to blame for first leading us to disobey God, thereby being the curator of shame. Satan acts by deception which leads to disobedience. The consequences of this rebellion manifest in our lives as shame.

Satan's Agenda

In the last chapter, I intentionally left out a primary character in the fall of humanity: The snake. The snake, also known as the serpent, is first introduced as craftier than any of the wild animals God had made. Some translations describe him as subtle, cunning, clever, sneaky, and skilled in deceit. Generally speaking, crafty and clever are positive attributes whereas sneaky and deceitful are perceived as negative traits. We must remember, though, that every piece of creation God made was good. Before sin, the created world was in perfect union with each other and with its Creator which brings into question the snake's actual purpose.

In Matthew 8:28, we read about a man who is demon-possessed, that is, a creation of God used by Satan for his purposes. Another instance in Job 1 shows Satan bargaining with God to torment Job's life. In an article from *The Gospel Coalition*, Richard M. Guy states:

> John Calvin argues that Satan chose the serpent as his mouthpiece because he knew that he couldn't appear to Adam and Eve and speak to them as himself. He needed a mouthpiece that wouldn't raise their immediate suspicions, one with which they would have been

familiar... He chose the one animal in all of God's creation that was most cunning or crafty (Gen. 3:1), the one that was the most shrewd or wise (Matt. 10:16).[5]

From the accounts in Matthew, Job, and Calvin, we can infer that Satan entered a harmless creature to approach Eve. The snake itself was not the devil or a symbolic figure. It was a snake that spoke to Eve, but he was only a mere instrument which Satan used to accomplish his purposes. So, from here on out, I will not refer to the serpent as the snake but as Satan.

Among all of the characteristics given to Satan, we will focus on deceit. *Collins Dictionary* defines deceit as "a behaviour that is deliberately intended to make people believe something that is not true."[6] In other words, Satan is an *expert* at making people believe lies.

Before Satan entered the body of the snake, his primary agenda was to make Eve believe that what God said was not true. It was not that he didn't know the truth, because to effectively tell a lie, the truth must be present. God's presence filled the garden, and before He ever spoke a word, He was the Word. Only the King of Lies can make us doubt God in spite of us being surrounded and created by truth.

Eve is forever our example as she was the first to encounter the skillful work of our enemy. Satan is just as cunning today as he was in the garden of Eden. Therefore, her experience allows us to map out his deceptive strategy toward us that leads us into repeated and often unintentional disobedience. The following are the three Ps of Satan's deceptive strategy:

1. He probes our knowledge.
2. He perverts our understanding.
3. He persuades our actions.

Probes Our Knowledge

We often think Satan is more powerful than he is. He exists under the authority of God and cannot create anything that is not already made, nor can he manipulate the truth. This means that the enemy's schemes toward us are rooted in what we already know and claim as our truth.

In Genesis 3:1 (NIV), Satan's first words to Eve were, "Did God really say, 'You must not eat from any tree in the garden?'" He could have skipped the mind games and told her to eat from the tree. Instead, he asked her a question that caused her to pause for a moment. What Satan was really asking was, "How much do you know about what God said?"

Have you ever been asked a really good question that forced you to think before answering? I imagine Eve fixing her mouth to quickly say, "Yes, that is what He said," only to realize she was not who received the instructions to begin with. Adam was the one that God directly ordered, which means it is likely that Adam could have told his wife exactly what God said or he told her only part of the commandment. In her defense, selective hearing is widely prevalent among the male species. Unfortunately, we are not told the details of their exchange, but it does give insight into why Satan approached Eve. Her vulnerability and lack of knowledge made her the perfect candidate to carry out his plan.

Eve responds in Genesis 3:2-3 (ESV): "We may eat of the fruit of the trees in the garden, but God said, 'You shall not eat of the fruit of the tree that is in the midst of the garden, neither shall you touch it, lest you die.'"

Dr. Richard Hess, professor at Glasgow Bible College in Scotland, comments on her response by stating:

> The woman's statement of God's qualification, forbidding the eating of the one tree, is interesting in what is changed. In 2:17 God identified this fruit as 'From the tree of the knowledge of good and evil you shall not eat.' However, the woman simply defines the fruit by the location of the tree: 'from the fruit of the tree which is in the midst of the garden God has said, You shall not eat.' By not defining the tree as one of good and evil, the woman has removed the reason for not eating from it. Bound up with the knowledge which this fruit conveys is the reason for the prohibition.[7]

Simply put, Eve responded to Satan in agreement that the tree was forbidden but she did not recall *the reason* it was forbidden. The location of the tree is insignificant compared to the differentiating characteristic of the prohibited tree. If Eve knew of the knowledge of good and evil, Satan would have less of a foothold because, remember, he cannot manipulate God's truth, only our version of it.

Ecclesiastes 7:12 (NIV) says, "but the advantage of knowledge is this: Wisdom preserves those who have it." God always has a reason for His rules. Whether we know them or not is a futile reason if we choose to obey; however, deception is almost inevitable when we forget God's exact words in the right context. Based on the lack of knowledge Eve possessed, Satan progressed with his plans to pervert her truth.

Perverts Our Understanding

Once our knowledge base is exposed, Satan then attacks our belief system. Our understanding of what we know is arguably more important than the truth. I have seen this time and again during Bible studies and small group discussions. After the text is read, each person goes around and says what they interpreted. I was leading a high school group once, and one interpretation was so far from the actual meaning of the passage that it took me several minutes to redirect the group. It is crucial to have an accurate understanding of God's commandments so that we are not vulnerable to Satan's attacks.

Satan further responded to the woman, "You will not surely die. For God knows that when you eat of it your eyes will be opened, and you will be like God, knowing good and evil" (Gen. 3:4-5 NIV).

Before this, Eve had no reason to doubt God's words or His commandments. She was sure of what she knew until Satan said similar words that sounded like what God originally said. Perversion is the alteration of something from its original course, also known as distortion.

Imagine standing in front of a broken mirror. Beyond the cracks, is the reflection still yours?

Yes.

Even though you can barely make out your features, have any of them changed?

No.

Does the broken mirror have any effect on reality?

Absolutely not.

Satan gave Eve a broken mirror, and he does the same to us. He slithers through whatever means are familiar to us to corrupt our faith. We intend well and wish to do honest work but our lack of knowledge and understanding of God's Word leads us to question Him. We start to doubt what He said, why He said it, and if it's actually true. And, when we are given an alternative picture of what could be, we are tempted to step outside the beauty of what already is.

Persuades Our Actions

The story proceeds in Genesis 3:6 (ESV):

> So when the woman saw that the tree was good for food, and that it was a delight to the eyes, and that the tree was desired to make one wise, she took of its fruit and ate, and she also gave some to her husband who was with her, and he ate.

Say what now?

Do you mean to tell me that Adam was right there the whole time? Why did he not interject and correct where Eve was wrong before it progressed? The people want to know.

This is the one time in history that mansplaining may have been acceptable, but we will leave that story for another day. The important and incredibly sad reality is that Satan's plans worked because the one commandment God had given humanity was broken.

Deception came.

Disobedience followed.

Shame erupted.

When we misunderstand what we think we know, our actions will follow. Eve saw that the tree was good and a delight, but she was light years away from the truth. She began to desire the lie that Satan offered her rather than deny the forbidden.

Eve is me, and her story is mine. Before the age of 15, I had no inclination to look at women lustfully. I thought the idea of homosexuality was silly since we all had the same parts and similar natures. As an athlete, we changed in front of each other all of the time, and there was not an ounce of attraction to any of them. I was almost too fixated on the boys coming out of the locker room with their white tee shirts and black gym shorts. If my middle school crush had professed his love for me, my story would have been much different. Not saying it would be one I am prouder of but different.

Satan knew this about me which is why he chose to slither same-sex attraction through my best friend, someone I already trusted, confided in, and loved. I would have immediately refused an invitation to hook up with a girl, but when my friend invited me into a deeper level of trust with her, it was not as easy to deny.

You see, it is so easy to judge Adam and Eve as we write them off so quickly with "they should've just obeyed," all while we are oblivious to our susceptibility to Satan's persuasive powers. They didn't plan to eat the forbidden fruit, Joe Branch didn't plan to become an alcoholic, and I didn't plan to be attracted to my friend, but it was all part of Satan's agenda. He will continue to slither, and we will continue to slip unless we prepare ourselves to combat his tactics.

Plan of Action

When you look back at your life and all of the times you disobeyed God, know that deception was at work. Like the two in the garden, each of us has been subject to Satan's agenda but our story does not have to end in defeat.

After humanity was broken, God made a promise that Eve's offspring will triumph over the enemy. Though the consequence of their sin led them out of the garden, God was sure to place an identity of victory over their lives. His words are never void of provision. In the same account from *Themelios*, Dr. Hess continues:

> The distortion of God's word is a misuse of God's gift. The motivation for that distortion is the desire to possess a full life apart from God's will. The result is the spiritual death of expulsion from the garden, with the consequent difficulties of coping in the resulting world.

Same-sex relationships are a distortion of God's gift of intimacy with another person. I know it feels right. She worships the ground you walk on, or he has never hurt you as other women have in the past. You're in love. The desire for love and intimacy were woven into us as we were made in God's image. The distortion, however, is with *who* and *how* we are living out those experiences. It is the same as a heterosexual couple engaging in premarital sex or someone abusing vulnerable children to fulfill a fantasy.

If we viewed God's commandments regarding sexuality as guardrails, we would be less inclined to drift into other lanes. Perversion never starts as a lie, but with some form of truth. This is why we must know God through His Word (Heb. 4:12). Not only should we know the facts but believe them and live it out (Jas. 2:14).

Questions are good, but they can also breed doubt. Sometimes it's good to take the Bible at face value. In simple terms, we obey because God said so. We are only here because God chose to breathe life into us and we cannot expect to experience the fullness of life outside of God's perfect design.

It is not too late for you to break the chain of shame over your life. Try not to think of all you expect to lose, like your relationships or affiliations with community groups. Just as I expected to be stoned to death by sharing my story with my Christian friend Kate, you may be pleasantly surprised at the type of embraces you receive once you release self-condemnation. Instead of expecting the worst, imagine a world free of shame where you are no longer a victim of deception. You are no longer entangled in lies or controlled by what others think. Imagine a world of tranquility, freedom, and joy where you are more than your sexual orientation, a place where your soul soars beyond the weight of depression and anxiety.

You do not have to wait until heaven to experience that kind of serenity. You can have a fullness of life here and now. Satan does not get to have the last word.

CHAPTER IV

RSVP

CHILDBIRTH IS KNOWN TO BE among the most beautiful phenomena of life. I have observed a few in nursing school, and though gory and intense, the joy of a new life is truly magical. While our clinical group was supposed to take note of the nurse's tasks during the delivery, I could only focus on two thoughts:

For it to be such a happy moment for everyone involved, why is the baby's first instinct to cry?

Moreover, why is the child, in their most innocent state, experiencing dissonance amid their new and welcoming environment?

Considering factors like the brightness of the room and the trauma during the birthing process, our common sense tells us that the child is uncomfortable. There is also scientific research that expounds on the physical changes that an infant encounters within the first few minutes of leaving the womb. It is undeniable that a child is physiologically imbalanced during their first moments post-delivery, but only to allow reasoning from a physical standpoint is superficial at best.

I believe the outcry of the infant is pointing to the spiritual imbalance within humanity. If you dare adjust your eyes to the dimmer light of childbirth, you will see that while life is a blessing from God, the cry of a child is evidence that the reality of our lives is marked by the curse of sin.

Ever since Adam and Eve were cast out of the garden of Eden, humanity has been living in exile. God's presence is our home, and though He is everywhere, our fallen flesh is the great wall between our spirit and soul. In the womb, our mother takes in food to feed our flesh, and in the same manner, the curse of sin flows out from her spirit and into ours. Again, even from my experience, I agree that hunger can make the most stoic adult cry, but it is dismissive to disregard the effects of hereditary sinfulness. The tears of a child serve as the hallmark sign of the homeless and helpless state of our souls. It should be all the evidence we need to know that something is not right.

Unfortunately, many have settled into this world like it is their forever. As for Christians, Earth is not our home. Most adults don't kick and scream when they are not immediately satisfied, but they do search for fulfillment elsewhere. Growing older does not remove our neediness, but we have only learned to distract ourselves from the true problem.

For example, if we walk outside without a coat and need to feel warm, we go back inside to cover ourselves. If we have a headache, we don't dwell in pain throughout the day. Instead, we take medicine to relieve the pain. If a person lay in bed for 24 hours, they would be hungry and thirsty, their throat dry, and their bed wet. If this were to continue, the person would eventually die from not tending to their bodily needs.

Am I suggesting that we stop taking care of ourselves?

No, but I am making the point that from the very beginning, we have been trained to immediately satisfy the longings of our flesh. All the while, our souls lay dormant and suffer from spiritual abandonment.

The umbilical cord being cut does not have to signify death and discomfort. Each child is born into the world of choice and free will. We can choose to live beyond our flesh. There is freedom in delaying instant gratification for the greatness to come. Once we realize we are spiritual beings as much as we are human beings, it will make a difference to our quality of life. If we only feed the human body, it will pass away along with this world. However, if we choose to nurture our spiritual body in Jesus, we will ascend to our heavenly home to be with our Creator again.

The Ground Is Level

Though I am a skeptic by nature, the idea of heaven has always been easy for me to believe. Some of my first thoughts of heaven were inspired by television. My parents built a collection of VHS tapes for my brother and me, and the one I would frequently grab was *All Dogs Go to Heaven*. In this movie, heaven had clouds that seemed plusher than my pillows, and the lighting was pink as if the sun never fully set, not to mention, cute pups flew around with wings. Another notable inspiration from television was *Touched by an Angel*. I watched this show with my mom, and rather than focusing on heaven as a distant destination, this show brought heaven to Earth. The angels were actual people like you and me. I have not resolved whether angels can enter the Earth as humans or if dogs will go to heaven, but I do know that heaven exists beyond our imagination.

Though heaven is known to be a faraway place, it has never felt inaccessible. I was confident that as long as I went to church, remained a good person, and asked for forgiveness when I sinned, then my soul was secure. It was not until I started to wrestle with same-sex attraction that I began to doubt my salvation.

When I went to college, I became involved with several Christian ministries. I had a lot of questions about my sexuality, so I took advantage of open-forum discussions. Because I never fully "came out," people did not feel the need to tip-toe around their words with me. I found that delicacies were not used in these discussions but rather a harshness that stemmed from hate. I was not ignorant of homosexuality being a sin, but people seemed to separate it from all other sins. A scripture that was often used was 1 Corinthians 6:9-10 (ESV):

> Or do you not know that the unrighteous will not inherit the kingdom of God? Do not be deceived: neither the sexually immoral, nor idolaters, nor adulterers, nor men who practice homosexuality, nor thieves, nor the greedy, nor drunkards, nor revilers, nor swindlers will inherit the kingdom of God.

I have visited many churches over the years. If I enjoy the Sunday service enough to visit three times in a row, I make it a point to attend the informational luncheon. Besides the opportunity for free lunch, it is a wonderful way to see behind the scenes and understand the "why" behind what they do. Most churches, if not all, have ministry groups that people can opt to join. They are usually smaller in size and connect people from various walks of life. The few I find myself most involved with are young adult groups, women groups, or singles ministry, but there are several more. I have seen groups for recovering alcoholics, couples who are dating, serving the homeless population, budgeting and finances, and groups for those addicted to pornography or drugs. Almost any person would feel safe in these environments, except for men who practice homosexuality.

Why is that?

How does a man who cheats differ from a man who suffers from greed?

How does a slave to alcohol differ from someone that makes an idol out of pleasing their family and friends?

How does a thief differ from an adulterer?

What allows for same-sex attraction to be isolated from the verse? How is it a less forgivable sin? And why does the church freely give a welcoming grace to those who struggle with other sins? It seems that people underneath the umbrella of homosexuality are withheld of grace as if the gates of heaven do not pour out salvation to all who believe.

I do not know the answers to those questions, but if I could take a wild guess, I would boil it down to one of two issues: Church people are ignorant to the biases they have of those who are queer, or they have never experienced the grace of God. What I mean by the latter is that many church people have based their salvation on their ability to live holy and do the right things apart from the work of the Holy Spirit. They look down on those dependent on God because they never had to be. Behold, this is the heartache of the misunderstood.

I wish that church people would pause for a moment and ask themselves about the point of ministry groups. If the purpose of a ministry group is to welcome those hurting and broken with hopes to share Jesus, they should be more concerned about which groups they should join than exclude others from them.

Whenever we buy into the notion that we have anything to offer people outside of Jesus, we have missed the mark. If for any reason, we believe we are the answer to people's problems, we must have forgotten that the church is Jesus' ministry. We are a work in progress with no room to judge or condemn. When the church fails to acknowledge their wretchedness and complete dependence on Christ, it unlevels the ground at Calvary.

If we are all honest, I think the look of drag kings and queens coming in and out of our "holy" spaces will force us to be uncomfortable. We fear we would say the wrong thing or look at them the wrong way. More so, we would have to massage out the cramps and knots in our hearts that keep us from loving them as Christ loves us. If we ignore them, exclude them from our list of groups, and pin a verse to keep them away, it would be much easier than learning the second greatest commandment: You shall love your neighbor as yourself.

Once I investigated the remainder of the verse in 1 Corinthians 6, I was completely taken aback by the clear omission of the next verse: "And such were some of you. But you were washed, you were sanctified, you were justified in the name of the Lord Jesus Christ and by the Spirit of our God" (1 Cor. 6:11 ESV). There is hope for the worst of sexual sinners, and His name is Jesus. How pitiful of a job are we doing as followers of Christ to obliterate Him from our ministry? How is it acceptable to allow our biases and lack of dependency on Jesus to bring condemnation on those who want to experience Him? Who are we to strip them of the salvation that Christ came to deliver?

To be a Christian and a recovering sexual immoralist, I find it very frustrating when attempting to share Christ with those I know. I want to invite them to church, but I know the trauma associated with it. I wish Christians embraced them as people while simultaneously pointing them to Christ. I don't know about you, but I want to rally everyone that I can to experience heaven as their home. Heaven will be free of bias. The walls of the flesh will come tumbling down, and our spirit and souls will be united with God once again. When Jesus came to Earth, He preached of the Kingdom of God being at hand, which indicates that heaven is not only a place to look forward to but an experience to live out in the here and now.

Bad and Good

Several places in scripture mention heaven as a kingdom. I find the best of Jesus' illustrations about the kingdom of heaven to be the Parable of the Wedding Feast (also called the Parable of the Great Banquet). It reads:

> And again Jesus spoke to them in parables, saying, "The kingdom of heaven may be compared to a king who gave a wedding feast for his son, and sent his servants to call those who were invited to the wedding feast, but they would not come. Again he sent other servants, saying, 'Tell those who are invited, "See, I have prepared my dinner, my oxen and my fat calves have been slaughtered, and everything is ready. Come to the wedding feast."' But they paid no attention and went off, one to his farm, another to his business, while the rest seized his servants, treated them shamefully, and killed them. The king was angry, and he sent his troops and destroyed those murderers and burned their city. Then he said to his servants, 'The wedding feast is ready, but those invited were not worthy' (Matthew 22:1-8 ESV).

In the story, God, the King, is throwing a party for His son, Jesus. With a Holy God as the host and the Messiah as the guest, this is not an ordinary event. Royalty is at hand, and those invited were considered high-calling. The Jews were the first group of people sent for by the servants. From Old Testament accounts, the Jews believed they were God's chosen ones and did not see themselves at the same level as the Gentiles. They were viewed as a prestigious lineage of people and would have fit in nicely at this party, but they chose not to come.

So, the king sent out his servants again, this time with a new marketing tactic. He described the menu, assuring them that this was not a cheap, finger-food gathering. He slaughtered animals and made sure the food was cleaned, prepped, and ready for them. Who can beat a five-star meal with no wait time? Yet, it was another unsuccessful attempt. Half of them chose their livelihood while others took captive the king's servants and killed them. The king immediately released his anger against these men and destroyed them and the town in which they lived.

The story takes a shift when the king tells the remaining servants that "those invited were not worthy" (Matthew 22:8 ESV). I imagine he took the scroll of the previously invited guests and ripped it to pieces. Even though those he originally called did not show, he was insistent that the feast be enjoyed.

The story continues:

> 'Go therefore to the main roads and invite to the wedding feast as many as you find.' And those servants went out into the roads and gathered all whom they found, both bad and good. So the wedding hall was filled with guests. "But when the king came in to look at the guests, he saw a man there who had no wedding garment. And he said to him, 'Friend, how did you get in here without a wedding garment?' And he was speechless. Then the king said to the attendants, 'Bind him hand and foot and cast him into the outer darkness. In that place there will be weeping and gnashing of teeth' (Matthew 22:9-13 ESV).

With the guest list ripped to shreds, the servants did not have any conditions regarding who they could invite. The only rule was that *everyone* was invited. It is a little strange that the first group of people was considered unworthy while the second group's invitation included bad and good people. We will circle back to that later.

The plot thickened as the king returned to the wedding hall to a party jumping with people. He must have been satisfied that the food was dwindling, and his son was properly celebrated, right? Well, not necessarily. The king scans the room and spots a man out of the dress code. The poor guy did not seem to get the suit-and-tie memo. Upon approaching him, all appears well as the king calls the man "friend." He proceeds to ask how he snuck past the bodyguards without the right clothes. It is not mentioned how much time he was given to answer, but the man stood silent.

The king's response was shocking. He instructed the man to be tied up and thrown out into the pit. Jesus finishes this suspenseful parable by saying, "For many are called, but few are chosen" (Matthew 22:14 ESV).

What in the world just happened?

Are you just as confused as I was when I first read that story?

Before we focus on the man who died, it is imperative to catch the distinction between those originally invited versus those who actually partook in the feast. The devout, religious, and successful were among the guest list. Their affluent titles and outward wealth made them appropriate invitees to such a noble event. In comparison to modern-day, each of us can think of someone we expect to go to heaven. Maybe we consider that someone to be ourselves. That person goes to church, knows the scriptures, and serves the poor. They are craftsmen of their trade with a picture-perfect family. *Oh, Mr. Jones? He is a blessed man.* But despite their qualifications, they make the choice not to go.

It seems weird that someone would openly deny the opportunity to go to heaven, but their choices are not as blatant as we would think. Some people surrounded by God-things choose not to believe God actually exists. They don't take scripture at its word or they would rather make idols of their earthly possessions. They have gotten comfortable with the constant praise from their boss and the conveniences of being wealthy. They think, *"That party may be fun, but I have all I need right here."*

The second half of the guests killed the king's servants.

The audacity!

Today's version of those guests is the people around the world that persecute Christians. They are also among the successful; however, they possess power and authority as well. God does not deal lightly with those who come against His own. Though there are governors, leaders, and kings, God is the ultimate king, and it is by His grace that He extended the invitation to them in the first place. By the obedience of faithful Christians, evil authorities still have the chance to be a part of God's kingdom. Without Jesus' covering, though, they are not spared His wrath.

Now let's take a look at the group of people who actually attended the king's banquet. There is not much to define them besides they seemed to be his last pick. One who reads this parable may even call the king desperate to have gone into the streets. It certainly makes me question his intentions, but despair is not a trait I observed. The temptation is to direct your attention to the guest list, but the focal point of the story is that the party is for the Son. When the King invites any and everyone, I see a Father more focused on his Son being celebrated than He is on the kind of attendants present.

Why?

Why does the Son matter?

Because there would be no need for the guests if it were not *for* Him.

In John 14:6 (NIV), Jesus says, "I am the Way, the Truth, and the Life. No one comes to my father, except through me." There is no access to the King if the Son is not present. There is no access to God if Jesus is not present. In the same light, there is no celebration of Jesus if there are no people to worship Him.

I hope to not do an injustice writing this as my heart is currently leaping for joy at this moment. In heaven, we will not be concerned about who else is there. If a murderer showed up or a rapist walked in, we would not know. Our gazes will be fixed on the guest of honor who will then direct our gaze to the Host. We have it all wrong if we think heaven is about us, our dogs, and fancy houses. None of that will matter because we will finally be reunited with our Creator. When we are birthed into heaven, we will not be babies crying from discomfort. Instead, we will be free of our flesh without tears, trauma, and temptations. All will be made right again and what a day that will be.

A Standing Invitation

Matthew Henry takes a stab at identifying the king's motive to cast out the improperly dressed man in his commentary of this parable. Henry alludes to the missing wedding garment to be the righteousness of Christ. The only guest *not* welcome is the guest found without the "righteousness of Christ and the sanctification of the Holy Spirit."[8]

Maybe you've rejected Jesus your whole life because you never knew what receiving Him actually meant. What makes life so beautiful is that as long as you are living, you have time. You can choose right now at this moment to receive all that Jesus is and what He represents. Part of receiving Jesus into your life is denouncing your self-sufficiency along with your attempts to attain your own righteousness. Isaiah 64:6 (NIV) says, "All our righteous acts are like filthy rags." You cannot make yourself holy since you were born with the DNA of sin, but you can start your journey to holiness after you receive Jesus as Lord.

Not only are you to receive Him, but you also are to believe in Him. You are to believe that Jesus was born through a virgin girl. As helpless as He was, He was still mighty and chosen. You are to believe that He was tempted by sin, but He did not sin. You must believe He innocently died a sinner's death, the death we deserved, and rose again from the grave, and that He is now seated at the right hand of God. Lastly, you are to believe in the miracles He performed. Yes, even Him walking on water. A key difference between receiving and believing is that your beliefs are rooted in what you value and who you trust. If your values align with Jesus' values, then your trust will soon follow.

God is not a respecter of persons. He wants His house to be full and He does not care about what baggage they bring. There is a standing invitation to heaven, yet the only way the invitation will go out is if Christians extend it. Scripture says, "And we all, with unveiled face, beholding the glory of the Lord, are being transformed into the same image from one degree of glory to another" (2 Cor. 3:18 ESV).

Below, I have written a *Declaration for the Church* that will serve as a prayer to remind us to set our perspectives on things above.

Declaration for the Church

I receive Jesus for who He is.
I believe all that Jesus did.
As the church,
I will be faithful in my role to extend heaven's invitation.
I will remember that no one is excluded.
I will not withhold God's invitation from those who desire to come.
I will aim to reflect the heavenly culture within the walls of my church.
I will not be found dressed in self-righteousness, but
when my garments become ragged,
I will go to the One who performs perfect alterations.
All is well now that I have a heavenly perspective.
If I forget, I will return to the ground of the Cross to be reminded.
I have sent in my RSVP.
My answer is yes, and yes forevermore.

CHAPTER V

Knock, Knock, Who's There?

I AM A VERY PRIVATE PERSON. I always have been. Even as a little girl, I would tell my mom to leave the bathroom when I needed to use the toilet. As I got older, I hardly ever changed in front of my friends or in the locker room. I preferred to use a stall. This never proved to be a problem for me until I went on an overnight field trip in middle school. Each hotel room was designated with one adult chaperone along with two to three students. The bathroom was a weird setup where you could access it from two different doors. Every time I used the toilet or shower, I would naturally lock both doors. Well, this is one of the first bathrooms I ever used with two separate doors. Once, after using the bathroom, I forgot to unlock the door to the chaperone's suite. I was made aware of this abominable behavior late one evening as we were all getting ready for bed.

Boom. Boom. Boom

Everyone in my room exchanged frightening glares, thinking the police were at the door.

Boom. Boom. Boom.

"Unlock the door now!" she shouted from her suite.

Apparently, we did not react soon enough because, in a blink of an eye, she was standing in our doorway with one towel on her head and another covering her torso. She was screaming at this point, "Why are y'all locking the doors? We all have the same parts and use the same bathroom! There's no reason to be locking doors here."

The loving woman who had been our lax chaperone became the big bad wolf over an action I thought was harmless. What about being locked out would cause her to bang on the door and scream like that? How had my request for privacy become offensive to her? Even after the situation settled down, and I explained to her that I had always locked the door when using the bathroom, she did not seem to understand. Being misunderstood hurts and it made me feel insecure.

From my standpoint, locking doors and changing in private had always made me feel safe from potential intruders. Especially living with my dad and brother, I wanted to protect myself and them from any accidental walk-ins. I also experienced body dysmorphia from time to time where I could hardly look at myself in the mirror without scolding the reflection staring back at me with cruel, nasty remarks. If I couldn't stand to see myself, I surely didn't want anyone else to see me in such a vulnerable state.

Thus, the door became the single greatest gift in my childhood and adolescence. I grew up seeing television shows where kids would put rules on their door, but that wasn't acceptable in my house. We didn't pay the bills so we couldn't declare rules. However, there was a mutual level of respect when my brother and I would bring certain requests to our parents. I only had two: knock before entering and shut the door when you leave. This placed me in control of who had access to me and when. It also allowed me to be at ease when I needed to shed layers, be it clothes or emotions, which made me susceptible to another's criticism. A closed door with me behind it made me feel safe. On the other hand, when my parents' door was closed, leaving me on the exterior, I felt left out and unwanted.

When you open the door of your heart to someone, you give them access to your very nature. They can do good or harm, bring you tears of joy or tears of sadness, and alter your life for the better or damage it for the worst. Although the easy answer may seem to be kicking the person out, it is not always so simple. Once we grant someone permission to see us, I mean really see beyond our superficial layers, we release the control we had when we were alone. Their reactions, words, and decisions impact us deeper than before.

In the opposite situation, when someone refuses to answer our knock, it can feel like an offense. How many times have you been locked outside the door of someone refusing to let you in? Maybe you're in danger on the outside and it's an urgent matter. Your life is threatened, and you need access to safety, or your loved one is in danger, supposedly threatening his life, and you are the rescuer. A closed door in a relational sense can feel like rejection, especially when a loved one starts withholding parts of themselves from you. You begin to spiral: *Why won't they talk to me? Why won't they hang out with me? What did I do wrong?*

Our position to a door makes a world of difference.

While living in downtown Oklahoma City, I bought a two-bedroom, two-bathroom unit, as I was anticipating a roommate to move in soon. Even while valuing my privacy, I recognized the sacrifices I needed to make to pay rent each month. In a few weeks, I found a roommate and she moved in quickly. We had a great relationship that extended beyond paying bills. She had become a friend that I grew to love and cherish. We started splitting groceries, sharing the responsibility of watching my dog, and exercising together. I felt so lucky to have scored a great friend as a roommate.

About two months later, it all hit the fan. We had a disagreement which led to her moving out way earlier than planned. One morning after work, I came home to a half-furnished apartment. Not only was she gone, and her things gone, too, but it felt like a part of me had also left. The life we shared no longer existed. It was back to me, my pup, and a whole lot of rent to be paid.

I share that story because I often think about what would have happened had I never let her move into my apartment. What if I kept the door closed to a girl who really needed a room at the time? Where would she have lived during those two months while facing extreme hardship and uncertainty in her life? What would have happened had I been unwilling to engage in a friendship with her? Would I have succumbed, once again, to depression while living in a new city by myself?

I don't know how the story would have turned out had I made a different decision. Once she came through that door, I had no control over whether she would leave or stay. The same is true for whomever you allow access to your secret hiding place. Opening the door is on you, but you were not given the authority to keep someone else hostage.

In the Closet

In the closet or "closeted" defined by *Urban Dictionary* is someone "who hides their true sexual orientation from the public and those around them, often for fear of persecution, rejection, or others' reactions."[9] The closet itself as the title of this book encapsulates the secrecy of living a life no one else knows. It is the life I lived for four years, although I would hardly call it living. I thought starting over in a new city after high school would provide the freedom I desired. The problem was that I did not know who I was or who I wanted to become. A glance and a coffee date had convinced most, if not all, that I was put together. I had every person in my life convinced, besides two people: Myself and God.

My closet, that is, the true me, was an entirely different story. As *Urban* defined it, I hid my true self from everyone around me. I was more than my good grades and friendliness. I was more than sunlit selfies and likable quotes. I was living in the darkest place of my life because I did not know my true self. Was I a curious lesbian who just wanted to test the waters? Was I bisexual because I was very much still attracted to men and wanted the traditional family structure? Was I a hypocrite for going to church and being a ministry leader while sometimes indulging in my sin?

You see, the thing about living a life in the dark is that no matter how hard you try to light it up by yourself or with the help of other people, it doesn't work. Darkness only breeds more darkness. An external light source must be present to truly illuminate our truth from the inside out. For a long time, I chose other people to act as lamps in my life. I use the word lamps intentionally because their joy, laughter, and good spirits could only brighten my day for a moment, but they also needed a match or a socket to turn on their light. And still, no human ever had enough watt power within to shed the weight of darkness from someone else. You will drain the people you care about the most if you place such an unattainable expectation on them.

It wasn't until I had lost every close person to me that I became aware of a new friend's interest. This one seemed to know where my secret place was exactly. He wasn't distracted by my external tidiness. In fact, he didn't seem fazed by it at all.

Knock. Knock. Knock.

To my surprise, this knock was completely different from my chaperone that night. It was more like a gentle thump, not rushed as if he were in danger nor rambunctious that would make me feel afraid.

Knock. Knock. Knock.

This person was unlike anyone I had ever known in that he was calm and consistent, never tiring of my stubbornness and resistance to let him in. It felt like he knew that I wanted to be found, discovered, and possibly even known.

Knock. Knock. Knock.

"Well, would you go away already?! I don't want company. I'll come out when I feel like it," I would internally pant. It made me sick to my stomach thinking of all the secrets I had buried away in there. I was not ready to be exposed. And yet again, *knock, knock, knock.*

Even in my hesitancy to open it, it made him no less patient.

No Face, No Case

As far as my child brain could fathom and my imaginative spirit could wonder, I have always believed in Jesus. I attended church and did church-like things. All was well until it wasn't. I was baptized at seven-years-old. Thirteen years later, while pursuing my bachelor's degree in nursing, I still felt like that same little girl asking myself the question my pastor asked me before I was submerged into the water: *Do you believe that Jesus is who He says He is?*

I had to finally admit that I didn't actually know who Jesus was outside of the people representing Him. I could point to who looked like what I thought Jesus was like, but I fell short in actually knowing Him personally. That was my downfall, and I strongly doubt I am alone.

In college, I had the opportunity to live in Orlando for a few months to deepen my faith and learn about evangelism. Each week, our big group would split into smaller groups to spread out across the city to share Jesus with others. It was most definitely my least favorite part of the week. I am an introvert through and through, so walking up to random strangers and asking if they think they'll go to heaven or hell was not something I ever looked forward to doing. Although, in doing this, my eyes were open to the widespread nature of spiritual darkness in our world.

If I could make it past my first question without being cursed out, the majority of people who walked away from God were because someone else misrepresented the person of Jesus. When I asked them what they knew about Jesus, I would often receive blank stares. Others would say something like, "I don't know about no Jesus, but there could be a God out there. I don't do church though."

"*How could this be?*" I thought. "*Can one believe in God and not the Bible or only certain parts of it? What do I believe?*"

Until I began to seek His face, I did not know that Jesus was the one knocking on my door. Being around people who allegedly acted like Him just wasn't enough anymore. Besides, how did I know they were being like Him if I didn't truly know Him? Talking to spiritual leaders are helpful at times, but you still run the risk of receiving opinionated and biased counsel. As Vern Poythress, a popular theologian and philosopher, once said:

> When we come to the Bible and try to listen to its claims, we can easily misjudge those claims if we hear them only from within the framework of our own modern assumptions. Letting the Bible speak for itself, that is, letting it speak in its own terms, includes letting the Bible speak from within its own worldview rather than merely our own.[10]

One of my favorite passages that describe the person of Jesus is found in the book of Isaiah. The prophet Isaiah made these accounts long before Jesus entered the world and they proved to be true throughout the Gospels in the New Testament. By dissecting Isaiah 53, I hope you see Jesus as the perfect companion in your closet space. He understands your struggle not only because He is God, but also because He experienced and defeated the same darkness in which you have been bound. Rejection is the common experience we share with Jesus. Scripture reads:

> For he grew up before him like a young plant, and like a root out of the dry ground; he had no form of majesty that we should look at him, and no beauty that we should desire him. He was despised and rejected by men, a man of sorrows and acquainted with grief; and as one from whom men hide their faces he was despised, and we esteemed him not (Isaiah 53:2-3 ESV).

I am no gardener, but I know not to expect plants to grow from dry soil. Plants need water and sunlight to have the slightest shot at surviving. Per my plant-mom friends, the process gets real fancy when you use specialized fertilizers. When treated properly, I have seen their small flowers and tiny cactuses grow as high as the ceiling. So, I had to pause at Isaiah's choice of words describing Jesus as a root out of the dry ground.

God breathed out life creating the very essence of biology as we know it, so how ironic that the entrance He chose into *His* created world was like a dried-up root? If "all things were made through him, and without him was not anything made that was made" is true as John 1 says, then what other reason would explain this?[11] Why not a tree planted by streams of water, as David described in Psalm, or like the burning bush that Moses saw in Exodus?

My first thought was that Jesus diminished His glory to match His environment. That is, He altered His true identity to fit in with the brokenness of the world. However, this could not be true once I studied the word "glory." The Hebrew definition of glory is heaviness or weight. A more common definition would describe glory as the summation of holiness, splendor, and majesty. John 1:14 (ESV) says, "And the Word became flesh and dwelt among us and we have seen his glory, glory as of the only Son from the Father, full of grace and truth." Jesus was not concerned with His environment any more than He wanted to alter His identity. In fact, He came so that we could see God's glory through Him.

On one hand, we have the prophet Isaiah foreshadowing that Jesus would grow up lacking splendor, beauty, and majesty in a form that no one would look His way. On the other hand, we have John's proclamation of the arrival of Jesus with special emphasis on the revelation of God's glory through Him. John anticipated that people in Jesus' time would catch a glimpse of God's glory simply by looking at Him. Either Isaiah or John was confused about how the glory of God would be manifested through Jesus as He entered the world, but then I realized they were both arriving at the same conclusion.

Regardless of how Jesus appeared to those around Him, it made Him no less glorious. He had no form of majesty and no beauty that we should desire, and yet He was still King and beloved by the Father (Jn. 3:16). The only difference in their accounts is the world's viewpoint versus heaven's viewpoint. Isaiah's focus is from the world's point of view. The Pharisees and Sadducees along with other townsmen rejected Jesus because of His appearance. I imagine they made comments like:

"Oh, that's just Jesus. Don't bother to look at him."

"Wasn't he born in a barn full of animals?"

"Didn't his mother have him out of wedlock?"

"His dad is just a carpenter."

They bypassed Him due to His earthly circumstances. Moreover, they did not accept Jesus because they could not see beneath the ground in which He was planted. Little did they know, underneath the soil was a ministry just waiting for God to water with His anointing.

Jesus did not come down from heaven to meet man's expectations. Jesus came down to Earth to restore God's expectations. Man could not take away from Him what they did not give to Him. The same is true for you. In all of the ways you have failed to meet the expectations of others for your life, Jesus has come to replace those with His own. He has more for you than a nice body and a pretty face. He desires you more than anyone ever could, leaving attraction to and for others irrelevant.

Let me reel you in: You are not who you are attracted to, and you are more valuable than what you attract. Nothing is wrong with you just like there was nothing wrong with Jesus. God wants to reveal to you the weight and heaviness of who He is through His Son, Jesus Christ. John 1:4-5 (ESV) reads: "In him was life, and the life was the light of men. The light shines in the darkness, and the darkness has not overcome it."

You can let Jesus in because He is the source of life, and He comes with light to outshine your present darkness. He has lived through rejection and has grieved the losses of relationships that could not accept Him for Him. He has felt the pain of being misunderstood. Jesus is knocking with a face lit with empathy, not judgment. Those reasons build a compelling case for Jesus as to why He is safe enough to enter your hiding place.

Access Granted

The story of Job is a classic example of how bad we misread situations. To paraphrase, Job was a God-fearing man who lived in an abundance of goodness. He was married with children and had an overwhelming amount of livestock. He was considered blessed and blameless by all who knew him until he lost everything he owned and became physically ill.

Among the arrival of his friends, they tried to comfort him but ended up making his situation worse. They ran out of consoling words, and they began to fault him for his mishaps. They viewed his suffering as a punishment from God, assuming he must have done something to receive such harsh treatment. The story ends with Job encountering God and being blessed with twice as much. There are many details I left out, so I hope that encourages you to read the full story.

Like Job, some people thought Jesus suffered because he was dealt a bad deck, that he must have deserved death if he was punished by way of crucifixion. Bad things cannot happen to good people, right? Wrong, but also that is not the point I'm aiming to make. The point is that Jesus did not willy-nilly live a hard life and die a sinner's death. He did it with you and me in mind. Matthew 27:27-31 (ESV) reads:

> Then the soldiers of the governor took Jesus into the governor's headquarters, and they gathered the whole battalion before him. And they stripped him and put a scarlet robe on him, and twisting together a crown of thorns, they put it on his head and put a reed in his right hand. And kneeling before him, they mocked him, saying, "Hail, King of the Jews!" And they spit on him and took the reed and struck him on the head. And when they had mocked him, they stripped him of the robe and put his own clothes on him and led him away to crucify him.

Jesus was stripped down and humiliated.
Jesus wore a crown of thorns on His head.
Jesus was mocked.
Jesus was spat on.
Jesus was bruised.
Jesus bled.
Jesus hung on a cross and died by suffocation.

He did it all so we do not have to. Yes, we were created with pieces of God's glory waiting to be revealed in us, but don't get it twisted—we have all turned away like sheep without a shepherd. We have chosen our own path rather than the one set for us. We have missed the mark of God's best for us. And because of this, we deserve the death that Jesus endured. It should have been us stripped down and humiliated. It should have been us with a crown of thorns. It should have been us who were mocked, spat on, bruised, hung on a cross to bleed, and eventually suffocated to death. That was our punishment. And still, while owing us nothing, Jesus stands at your door and knocks. If anyone hears His voice and opens the door, He will come in.[12] Don't miss the opportunity to know Jesus in this light. It is a personal and powerful experience that has eternally changed my life.

In the following chapters, there are practicals to following Jesus, but they will have no lasting effect if you don't first reconcile your heart to Jesus. No pressure, though. His knock is unrushed.

CHAPTER VI

Yes, You!

WITH SIX SECONDS left on the clock until the half, my teammate inbounded me the ball underneath the opponent's goal. We were down by 11. I dribbled as far as I could, just shy of the half-court line, threw up the biggest prayer of my life, and the ball was all net. The crowd went *wild*.

I wasn't one of those kids who grew up with a basketball in my hands. I started "hooping," as true ballers call it, in eighth grade, and boy did my coach take a chance on me. I had a lot of raw talent, but I lacked coordination and basic knowledge of how the game worked. Needless to say, my middle school coach made me a post-player who never had to dribble down the court or shoot from behind the free-throw line. I hardly ever played in games, so my time to shine was cracking jokes at practice which inevitably sent me to the sidelines running suicides while everyone else learned our plays.

It wasn't until I received "Most Improved Player" at our end-of-the-year basketball banquet that I started to believe I could be more than the clumsy class clown. If I took the sport more seriously, I could continue to improve and possibly make the high school team. Looking back at my journey, that half-court buzzer shot meant so much more to me than impressing the crowd. I had sacrificed the time to perfect my skills which brought me from post player to point guard, and most importantly, I learned the art of believing in myself.

The next half of the game was probably the best basketball I ever played. Our team came out with a new momentum that quite literally put the tempo and speed of the game in our hands. The other team was noticeably offset by our comeback. Unfortunately, we came up short by two points, and as unusual as it was for a competitor like me, I walked off the court content.

I remember the energy of the locker room that night like it was yesterday. We always had about five or so minutes to celebrate, pout, or say whatever was on our minds before our coaches would come into the locker room. As a captain of the team, I was very aware of my body language. I never wanted to overreact or lose my temper in front of the girls, leaving a poor example of sportsmanship. That night, though, I was partying with everyone else. The loss didn't affect us like others because of the cohesiveness we showed as a team. We lost so many games before this that I thought we would never find our groove. I was hopeful that my senior year would be better than the last three years, and if I continued to play with the same initiation and control that I just showed, I could have a shot at playing at a junior college upon graduation.

Our assistant coach walked in first to make sure we all were dressed, and then entered our head coach. Per usual, we sat down, anticipating his spiel—first, the highs and lows of the game. Then, individual areas of improvement, and finally, the time and date of our next practice. I could have sworn I was listening attentively unless my mind wandered to the jalapeno-covered nachos that I often thought about after games. I heard him say that the team would benefit if I dribbled with my head up, and how another player should box out. The night was just another night until it wasn't. Out of nowhere, a small voice spoke to me and said, "Choose me." I looked around to see if anyone else heard it.

Nope.

Just me.

Great.

I felt a pit in my stomach, thought I was just imagining things, and tried to catch up to speed on what the coach was saying. Then again, I heard, "Choose me."

The second time, I knew it was God, and I knew exactly what He meant by those words. Just a few months before the beginning of my senior year, I was emotionally wrecked. My best friend at the time, who I loved like a girlfriend, she and I were officially on break. I had no idea how to do life without her. We did everything together. My life was so deeply rooted in hers that I only saw myself to the extent of how she viewed me. When things were great, I was funny, smart, beautiful, and invaluable. When we were at odds, I was the worst in every way possible. Whatever profane word that came to your mind, I was all that and the next word, too. It was hard for me to find purpose in living if we weren't together.

The first few weeks into our break were Earth-shattering. I would just lie in bed in my dark room and hold my pillow. I even Googled "does heartbreak make your heart physically hurt?" I was convinced that death was summoning me. Scientifically, adolescents' brains have not developed enough to properly contextualize their feelings. In other words, I had not experienced enough yet to know that relationships don't last forever, and seeing her less would not actually kill me. At the time, you could not convince me otherwise. So, as dramatic as it sounds, I was physically without energy, mentally without motivation, and emotionally dead.

I missed our time together, but I began to pick up the pieces little by little as the summer went on. Senior year was approaching, and excitement for the next phase of life began to consume my thoughts. Before I knew it, school was back in session, and as much as I tried to pick up where we left off, the joy I anticipated was not there anymore. The break was the gracious rehabilitation I never knew I needed. Unlike the famous quote, time apart did not make my heart grow fonder.

Many blind spots in our relationship became a lot more visible once we were together again—the way we would tear each other down just to build each other up made me wonder how I did this for ten months or the fact that we both had cut everyone else off besides each other. I remember sitting in a senior class meeting one day, completely bemused at how I lost touch with some of my best friends in ninth and tenth grade.

Where had they gone or was I the one that left?

As time went on, being with her made me feel more detached from who I wanted to be. I didn't know all that I wanted for myself, but I did know I wanted more. I wanted more stability, more friendships, and more wholeness. I also wanted less hiding, less emotional plummets, less anxiety, less fear, and less doubt.

The last time I prayed, I asked God why He allowed the relationship to happen in the first place, and there I was, almost a year later, asking Him if He would give me a way out. I didn't hear anything the first time I prayed, so I felt silly to expect a response now. My prayer sounded something like:

> *Hey, God. I need a way out, preferably one that would not lead to humiliation by her outing me to the school. Also, can we somehow remain friends even though we are already friends? I don't know. You know what I mean… like, actual friends.*

Since the very beginning of this closeted relationship, I had been staring at the door, wondering when I would come out and what that come out would look like. In the locker room that night, after the greatest game I'd ever played and undoubtedly the most important year of my basketball career, God answered my prayer with a quiet voice asking me to choose Him, and though He never said to quit the basketball team, I knew that was exactly what He meant. He was offering to be my rescue if only I trusted Him enough to surrender the idols of my heart.

I thought, *"But God, can she not quit the team? Why me?!"*

He said nothing.

Frustrated and confused, I slowly started to place my shoes in my bag, then my ankle braces. At this point, my coach stopped talking, and I felt burning holes all over my body as if my teammates' eyes were beaming lasers through me. I kept packing until I had everything I brought, besides the clarity I thought I had for my future. I looked at no one and walked out of the locker room for what would be the last time.

Oddly, my mom was at the top of the stairs as I was walking up, and I lost it. Between the tears, I tried to explain what I had no explanation for. I loved the game of basketball. I had spent countless hours trying to perfect my skill just so I could be decent enough to compete at the next level. In fact, I just had a conversation with my assistant coach that same week about post-grad opportunities. In a matter of moments, none of it mattered as I was walking away from it all with no plan B. I didn't stay for the boys' game or speak to anyone on the way out of the door. I walked to my car and tried to stop crying long enough to get home safely.

In Genesis 15, there is a story of a man named Abram who desired an heir but was discouraged by his old age. God gave him a vision by the night sky that as many stars as Abram could count would be the number of generations that would succeed his own son. In chapter 16, Abram's wife, Sarai, was sure that God cursed her from having children, so she sent her servant, Hagar, to Abram to become his wife. When Hagar became pregnant, Sarai loathed Hagar and began to treat her poorly (v.6). Hagar fled (v.8), but God sent her back to Abram and Sarai where she bore Abram's first son, Ishmael (v.15).

When Abram was 99 years old, God spoke to him again, reiterating His promise, but this time changing Abram's name to Abraham and Sarai's name to Sarah (Gen. 17:1-5;15). Ishmael was not the son God promised to inherit Abraham's kingdom, but Sarah would bear the promised son even in her old age. When Sarah caught wind of this promise, she laughed (Gen 18:15). A year later, Sarah gave birth to a son named Isaac, and God's promise to Abraham was fulfilled (Gen 21:5).

Before God appeared to Abraham, Abraham had already decided that someone else in his family would receive his inheritance. In Abraham's eyes, his age made him ineligible from having his own son. Sarah also assumed her age and barrenness disqualified her from the promise God spoke over her. In an attempt to make sense of God's promise, Sarah begrudgingly denounced her marriage to her servant as if God told her to do so. She let go of a good thing and God didn't even tell her to do that. She then took out her frustration on the poor servant who only obeyed her instructions. In Sarah's defense, it would be difficult for anyone to believe that their future hinged on a promise that had not yet been conceived. And still, she was called to trust God's words despite her present reality.

How often do we confuse trust with sacrifice?

We often believe that to trust God at His word is the equivalence of letting go of everything good He's already given us. Sarah had a good thing with Abraham, but because her mind was tunneled by her ability to fulfill God's plan on her own, she was quick to act, even if it was a poor decision. Had Sarah simply waited on God to move, Hagar would have continued servant-like duties without the added drama of becoming a mistress. With a displaced fixation on sacrifice, Sarah limited God to two options: Abraham would not have an heir because of her barrenness, or that the heir would need to come from someone else. When we make ourselves the main character in our own story, we strike out option three that only the real Main Character writes in for us.

God's third option for Sarah was for her to trust Him to fulfill His promise through means that only He could provide. The same is for us. The plans that God has for us are only made accessible when we choose to trust Him. Unfortunately, those plans are often not detailed to us, and even if they were, we would laugh as Sarah did. He carries out His plans from an entirely different realm of resources that our hands cannot access. Though God has placed a different purpose within each of us, His ultimate plan for us is salvation, not by sacrifice, but by trusting Him.

I thought for many years that quitting basketball was the sacrifice God required for me to truly receive salvation, and if I had not responded to His voice at that particular moment, I would not be where I am today. I could not have been further from the truth. Jesus' death was the only sacrifice efficient enough to pay our indebtedness to sin, so God is not asking for anything that we have in our possession. God actually wants us to surrender ourselves and acknowledge that we are His possession. Choosing God over basketball and my previous relationship was less about me giving them up and more about giving myself back to Him.

You, too, may be reluctant to believe you can have a relationship with Jesus because of what you are unwilling to release right now at this exact moment but your salvation is not contingent upon you or the secrets you carry. Ephesians 2:8-9 (ESV) assures us, "For by grace you have been saved through faith. And this is not your own doing; it is the gift of God, not a result of works so that no one may boast."

Salvation is God's thing and surrendering is our thing. God is many things, but above all, He is self-sufficient which means He is not dependent on anyone else.

> For by him all things were created, in heaven and on earth, visible and invisible, whether thrones or dominions or rulers or authorities– all things were created through him and for him (Colossians 1:16 ESV).

If every human were eradicated today, the Earth and all of its beauty would live on. God created the entire universe and everything in it before He made Adam and Eve which means it was never *for us* but *for Himself.* As part of His creation, we, too, were created for His pleasure and delight.

If God wants a relationship with you, He has a plan to do just that and there is nothing you can do about it.

It can feel very confusing to wrap your mind around a God that wants a relationship with you in your current condition, especially when you have experienced church cultures that claim to love Jesus but blatantly shunned you. The disconnect is real, and it is normal to think you are better off without any of it. At the peak of my rebellion, I convinced myself that heaven and hell were not real places just to help me sleep at night. The thought of God being real and knowing I had no relationship with Him was too sobering, and the constant rejection from homophobic Christians was too disheartening. There were few resources to help me sort through my thoughts. So, denying God altogether was the easiest choice.

I don't know your exact situation, but I do know that your denial of God's existence is a sure sign that your heart has been hardened toward Him. You may have experienced a misrepresentation of God's heart from Christians, or you have experienced several difficulties in life that led to you doing life without Him. The worst part of denial, though, is that truth prevails, and the world you have created for yourself, apart from the acknowledgment of God as the true Creator, is just an illusion. In the same way that your hurt is tangibly real, so is God's desire to be with you and heal your bleeding heart. The work has already been done through Jesus. While we were still sinners, He chose to not only die for us but to resurrect, that we can have a chance at the new life He came to bring.[13] It is only up to us to surrender by choosing to believe Him and follow His lead.

Make no mistake: There are places in your life that God wants to take you (yes, you!) not because of your deservingness but because He is a merciful God. When He speaks, His words cannot return to Him empty.[14] God's promise to you is about making good on His promise to Himself. With the same attitude that God spoke to Moses is the same in which He speaks to you:

And the Lord said to Moses, "This very thing that you have spoken I will do, for you have found favor in my sight, and I know you by name." Moses said, "Please show me your glory." And he said, "I will make all my goodness pass before you and will proclaim before you my name 'The Lord.' And I will be gracious to whom I will be gracious, and will show mercy on whom I will show mercy (Exodus 33:17-19 ESV).

Go With the Flow

The art of humanity is that we are complex beings. Self-expression is our best attempt to be understood and tell our unique stories. We go to great lengths to make sure people know who we really are and even greater lengths to conceal the parts of ourselves we wish we were not. Identity is everything and even those outside of the LGBTQIA+ community struggle to conquer the restrictive labels that society has placed on them. For example, a Black man in America works twice as hard not to end up in prison or dead. Also, a Caucasian woman presumably does not want to be a "Karen" for calling customer service. When constantly fighting to prove who we are to the world, we fail to let God aid us in understanding who we are to become.

When we look back at Abraham and Sarah's story, their names had to be changed before they could receive God's promise. Note that they received a vision of God's promise while they were Abram and Sarai, and it was only after God gave them their new identities that He fulfilled His plan for them. God's covenant with Abram was much different than the new covenant with Abraham. Abram's vision was a bit hazy. He could not clearly see how God would bring him a son, so he did not oppose when Sarai encouraged him to be with Hagar. It was not until he was Abraham that he was declared a father of nations with kings in his bloodline. God made clear to him then that his son would not be from Hagar or the previous version of his wife Sarai. Further, Sarai's name would also need to be changed to Sarah to bear the promised child.

The version of you who has not had an encounter with Jesus is not the version of you that will walk in the fulfillment of God's calling for you. God wishes to reveal His glory to you, but a transformation must occur first. You can no longer be associated with the narrative you have written for yourself. Instead, you must be willing to surrender your authorship to God and allow Him to narrate your story by rewriting your character.

Paul says that "we are God's workmanship, created in Christ Jesus for good works, which God prepared beforehand that we should walk in them" (Eph. 2:10 ESV), so wouldn't it make sense for us to let God reveal to us what He has already written rather than attempting to rewrite our own bootleg copy? The thing about bootleg movies is that they are free, but they lack the wow effect that the actual in-theater movie experience brings. The same is true with our version of our story versus God's version. When we cut corners, we sell ourselves short by only dreaming of what life could be instead of living the sensational experience of God's story in 4D. The cost difference is forgoing our path and allowing Jesus to lead us.

Regardless of what you previously observed from Christians, following Jesus is as literal as it sounds. I wish more people would identify as Christ-followers as a reminder of what we're doing and why we're doing it, but I digress. In the Gospel of John, Jesus uses a compelling analogy about a shepherd and his flock and how we are to let him lead us.

> "I am the good shepherd; I know my own sheep, and they know me, just as my Father knows me and I know the Father. So I sacrifice my life for the sheep. I have other sheep, too, that are not in this sheepfold. I must bring them also. They will listen to my voice, and there will be one flock with one shepherd" (John 10:14-16 NLT).

Sheep will wander off a cliff if they do not have a *good* shepherd leading them. I emphasize the word "good" because Jesus mentioned earlier in this same parable that others have come to attempt to lead his flock with poor intentions for the sheep.[15] Heed this warning: You are following someone, whether a person, institution, or ideology. Someone or something is guiding your steps and it can be detrimental to your life if you are not cautious. Jesus is boldly claiming that He is the good shepherd because He died for His sheep. One will scarcely die for a righteous person but Jesus died for us all. Every single one of us.[16]

Did you notice the shift in verse 16 as Jesus makes a special note of going after sheep that are not already in His sheepfold? Unlike many churches, Jesus was not content with the multitudes that were already following Him, nor was He concerned if the sheep were a different breed with a dingier coat. As the shepherd, Jesus always has an eye looking outward so that He can gather those who are not already on the inside. Jesus is pursuing the current version of you hiding and fearful of others' opinions.

Yes, you who have walled yourself off from the church.

Yes, you who are still doubting your worth.

Yes, you who have been denied and cut off from your family.

Jesus has already laid down His life for you so you can become part of the greater body of Christ. The act of following Jesus begins passive as Jesus has been pursuing you long before you noticed, but once you become aware of His pursuit, you must make an active decision to stay within the flock. That is, continue to go with his flow wherever he has already been leading you. David says in Psalm 23 that those who allow Jesus to lead them shall not want (v. 1). Their crushed souls will be restored (v.3). Even when darkness prevails, Jesus' company will provide comfort and cast off fear (v.4). Those who hurt them will witness their transformation and be amazed by God's anointing on their life (v.5) and His goodness and mercy will follow them the rest of their days (v.6).

The journey with Jesus is not all rainbows and butterflies, but my experience has proven it to be far better than a life without Him. Sacrifices are not a means by which salvation is attained, but to follow Jesus, we must be willing to release what pulls us in the opposite direction in which He leads. Releasing is hard, and you may never understand why, but I hope you find comfort in knowing that Jesus is calling you out of hiding. Yes, you! Even with the billions of sheep He is already herding, He still wants you.

Repeat this after me:

I am important.
I am necessary.
I am wanted.
I am loved.
I am called.
I am chosen.
I have a promise.
I will not stay in hiding.
I will come out.

Chapter VII

Our Better Half

How would you feel if you were sent to a camp at 13 years old after coming out to your parents about your sexuality? It wouldn't be just any camp but one whose purpose was to cast out the gay in you, and if you did not flip the magical switch that conveniently turns homosexuality on and off, you could be subjected to electroshock or food deprivation. At the very least, you would be made to feel like an abomination to God and a disappointment to the loved ones who sent you there. If you had the privilege of knowing this beforehand, would you come out?

As much as I wish that experience is made up, it is not. Conversion therapy has been practiced since the 1890s with the sole purpose of changing one's sexual orientation or gender identity and is rooted in the belief that same-sex attraction is abnormal. Conversion camps were often hosted by religious leaders who would gather groups of openly or suspected gay adolescents and attempt to preach, pray, or cast out the demon allegedly living inside of them. Adult survivors of these camps have spoken out about these monstrous events done to them in childhood and are still scarred from the torture inflicted upon them. The following are some of their statements:

"They [the camp leaders] were saying I was demon possessed and going to hell."

"It made me feel ashamed for many years that you don't feel like a human."

"When I was prayed for, it was lengthy, it was loud, it was two adults shouting and pushing down on my head, forcing me to my knees."

According to the UCLA School of Law, as of 2019, nearly 700,000 adults had received conversion therapy in their lives, and more than half of that number were under the age of 18 at the time of the treatments.[17] *The Journal of Child and Adolescent Psychiatric Nursing* showed that LGB adolescents' relationships with their parents are often challenged, particularly around the time of disclosure of sexual identity or "coming out" and found a staggering correlation between parental rejection during adolescence and the use of illegal drugs, depression, attempted suicide, and sexual health risk by LGB young adults.[18]

Though conversion camps have been banned and are illegal in most states, it has not stopped underground activity, nor has it eradicated the belief that those in the LGBTQIA+ community have pathological illnesses requiring some form of treatment. Those biases have been passed on for generations, that many outsiders subconsciously hold those beliefs and are completely unaware of the discrimination they inflict on this community. Though the shame that many closeted individuals carry is caused by others, it is often an internal battle with themselves as a result of the environment in which they were raised.

As I watched the videos and read the stories of the people who were courageous enough to share their traumatic experiences, I was burdened with mixed feelings. While becoming inspired by the resilience of those who fought to keep living after explicit mistreatment from the church, I couldn't help but mourn those who gave up altogether. The reality is that these actions from religious entities are not things of the past but an ongoing problem. The Bible has been used as a weapon to persecute children and adults who have not met the vanilla, cookie-cutter version of the ideal Christian. All too often, religious leaders have stood from elevated platforms, pronouncing same-sex attraction to be an unforgivable sin that immediately warrants the outpouring of God's wrathful judgment, refusing to acknowledge that His mercy is for *all* who believe. The same has been true for parishioners as they sit silent, completely ignoring the lack of outreach to the LGBTQIA+ community. All degrees of such behavior are despicable and have perpetuated the act of foreclosing masses of people to spiritual homelessness. We must come to realize that matters of condemnation and conversion are part of heaven's conversations. They are not horizontal matters that man should spend their time grappling with.

If you are in the process of healing the aforementioned soul wounds or similar traumas, remember that if you believe in the redemptive work of Jesus and have surrendered your life to Him, you are no longer the author of your story. Jesus is the author and perfecter of your faith.[19] Because of His sacrifice, you are now considered a chosen people, a royal priesthood, and a holy nation that you may declare the praises of Him who called you out of darkness into His wonderful light (Pet. 2:9 NLT). God knew you'd have the desires that you do before He created you, so though you may have surprised yourself and your community by openly acknowledging your sexual preferences, God is not surprised and already has a plan to redeem *His* calling for your life.

Also, remember the true villain of your story is Satan and he is set on taking you out.[20] He is the demon, not *you*. His deception and lies have infiltrated humanity with a nature of disobedience, and though you have tried to stop the cycle of sin in your life, Satan is not letting you go that easy. You did not fall through the cracks of heaven and mistakenly land on Earth. You are meant to be here, and God wants to give you a life free of shame and full of purpose. Learning to discern what is God and what is Satan is essential to a life of freedom. Thankfully, we were not left to our own vices to do so.

Up until now, we have seen how God's plan from the very beginning was to restore our relationship with Him by sacrificing Himself through His Son. The bridge from our closet back to God is through Jesus, but the story does not end there. God anticipated we would need help navigating the post-closet life, and because Jesus' flesh limited His time on Earth, He chose to continue dwelling with us but this time from the inside.

The remaining chapters of the book will focus on the third person of the triune God, the Holy Spirit. The Holy Spirit is the *only* agent by which we possess the freedom to live as we are while transforming into someone new. If we acknowledge His presence, He will help us discern truth from lies, right from wrong, and freedom from bondage. Unlike man's attempts to convert groups of people by tormenting and exiling them from the church, the presence of the Holy Spirit actually unifies the body of Christ by transforming each of us into the same image from one degree of glory to another.[21] He is truly our better half, taking us from bad to good, good to better, and better to best by moving in three specific ways:

1. He frees us from the need to be perfect.
2. He replaces old desires with new desires.
3. He equips us with the tools needed to fulfill His purpose for our lives.

Denouncing Perfectionism

Perfectionism is a fear-based mechanism that places shackles on the areas of our lives where God wants to provide freedom. Along the lines of spiritual growth and maturity, it is quite easy to adopt a thought pattern that tells you that you must do all the right things in the right way to be a good Christian:

Don't steal.

Don't lie.

Don't cheat.

Don't sleep with the same gender.

Don't change your biological anatomy.

Don't complain.

Don't. Don't. Don't. The don'ts never stop and neither do the dos. I spent so many years of my faith journey trying to be perfect that I missed the essence of God's grace. I don't want that for you. Grace is God's free gift of unmerited goodness to each of us. There is no means by which we could attain this level of goodness on our own.

Here is an analogy: A transplant recipient needs a new heart, but their condition leaves them powerless to attain one for themselves. There is a standard procedure by which recipients are listed, and no matter how much they cry, kick, or scream, the laws are set. In the same way, our hearts are spiritually sick, and we are desperately in need of a new one. Religion has a set of laws, or commandments, that outline the hoops we must jump through to receive our new heart. Due to the strict dos and don'ts, it is impossible to meet the criteria for a suitable donor. Grace, on the other hand, is God's reform to this broken religious system. Jesus is the only suitable donor for a new heart, and by His death, we were given the Holy Spirit who performs a heart transplant on us.

Another picture of grace is through the story of Paul. If you have never heard of Paul, here's the rundown. Saul, who we know now as Paul, was a man who hated Christians. He was a lot like those people who tell you that God doesn't love you and you're better off in hell except Saul skipped the chit-chat. He was a cold-blooded killer to those who followed the teachings of Jesus. He was on the ultimate killing spree before God stopped him in his tracks by an angel, changed his name, and set him on a new path to preach to the very people he once despised. So, if anyone knows grace, it's our boy Paul.

After Paul's conversion, he unsubscribed to the law of man and chose to live by the standard of God. He says in Galatians 2:20 (ESV):

> I have been crucified with Christ. It is no longer I who live but Christ who lives in me. And the life I now live in the flesh I live by faith in the Son of God, who loved me and gave himself for me.

Paul realized that to receive his new heart, he had to let go of his old life. Ephesians 2:1-3 (ESV) says:

> And you were dead in the trespasses and sins in which you once walked, following the course of this world, following the prince of the power of air, the spirit that is now at work in the sons of disobedience—among whom we all once lived in the passions of our flesh, carrying out the desires of the body and the mind, and were by nature children of wrath, like the rest of mankind.

We all lived in the passions of our flesh at one point or another, but you can choose right now to die to your old life and embark on a new journey. The key to living a life full of grace is your willingness to yield to this new life with Christ. Free will gives you the choice to be led by the Spirit or to continue to bow down to the laws of perfectionism, which is unattainable and a lot less enjoyable. 2 Corinthians 12:9 (ESV) says, "My Grace is sufficient for you, for my power is made perfect in weakness." When you acknowledge the fact that you are not perfect and will never attain perfection on your own, you can live freely in the areas where you are weak because you know the Holy Spirit is at work inside of you.

Some of you will make room for the Holy Spirit to enter into your life, and the transformation will be instant as with Paul. For others, like myself, your transformation will be a gradual process that will lead you to question if you ever received the Holy Spirit. Your desires will still feel as strong as they were, and you will sometimes grieve the old version of yourself, making it very tempting to go back.

Don't.

In due time, you will begin to see tangible results from the Holy Spirit's work. You will become acquainted with your new friend living inside of you and adapt to the timing of His ways. As long as you live on Earth, your heart surgery will remain in progress but the freedom of embracing your weakness is far better than living a performative life of perfectionism.

Breaking Strongholds

I am not one of those "New Year, New Me" types of people. I don't create vision boards, nor do I choose a special word to mark the next 12 months. Before you write me off as pessimistic, I have a particularly good reason for this.

Over the course of my battle with same-sex attraction, I would tell myself, "This is the last year I'm doing this." Every year, I crossed my fingers, closed my eyes, and blew out my birthday candles, wishing the gay away. After manifesting newness for five consecutive years, I resigned from the tradition. I was confused by God for allowing me to fall in love with the first girl, and I was more frustrated with Him for allowing similar situations to arise in college. When I ended the relationship in high school and gave my life to Christ, scripture promised I would become a new creation.[22] I thought following Jesus would help me to be free of those desires, so when I found little to no progress after entering into a relationship with Him, I began to lose hope. I can bet the house that I don't have that you relate to these sentiments. I know, for sure, Paul can relate. Read what he wrote in Romans 7:15-19 (ESV):

> For I do not understand my own actions. For I do not do what I want, but I do the very thing I hate. Now if I do what I do not want, I agree with the law, that it is good. So now it is no longer I who do it, but sin that dwells within me. For I know that nothing good dwells in me, that is, in my flesh. For I have the desire to do what is right, but not the ability to carry it out. For I do not do the good I want, but the evil I do not want is what I keep on doing.

As Paul says in verse 18, my problem was not that I did not have good desires, but that I did not possess the ability to carry out those desires on my own. That is my issue with most New Year's resolutions. When we set goals to break old habits and start new ones, we often fail to acknowledge the One who enables us to do so. Habits are the outward presentation of the inward desires of our hearts. In other words, once our desires change, our habits will follow, and the Holy Spirit is the only one who can give us new desires.

In Leviticus 11:45, God calls the Israelites to be holy because He is holy. Holiness is the state of being like God or being set apart, and it fuels our spiritual discipline. In the same way that a sick heart cannot regenerate a healthy heart, neither can one discipline themselves into holy living. For example, how many times have you set the goal to wake up early in the morning to start your day by reading the Bible? The first few weeks, maybe even months, may go well but you eventually find yourself setting the goal again. And again. And again. Discipline causes you to wake up at a set time each morning, but the yearning to actually read the Bible comes from the Holy Spirit living inside of you.

If you think that good desires equate to a boring life, I used to think that too. Here's the thing: When we are full of sewage, we can't appreciate the benefit of clean water. The Holy Spirit cleans us out by giving us a constant source of purified water, but if you've ever poured a cup of water into a cup of dirt, it will get messy. The same is true with us. You won't instantly feel clean because the dirt from living in disobedience for years has accumulated all kinds of filth in the tightest of spaces. It will take constant flushing by the Holy Spirit to reach those grimy areas and sustain your appetite for what is pure. Eventually, disobedience will become as foreign as obedience once was in your life. You will begin to crave the things of God and despise the ways of the world.

In the event that you've already been washed by the Holy Spirit, but you still feel that there's some sin you just can't rid yourself of, you are more than likely bound by a stronghold. A stronghold is an oppressive form of sin that is not easily broken from your life. I'm not talking about the stronghold that chocolate cake or a large McDonald's fry has on you at 2 a.m. I'm referring to the grip Satan has on your soul through the passions of your flesh, whether greed, lust, pride, or hate, to name a few, the type of grip that leads you to repeat the same mistakes with the same types of people and eventually pass those same patterns to future generations. Fighting strongholds in your own strength will leave you feeling defeated and hopeless.

Historically, there is only one account of a man powerful enough not only to break the stronghold of death but to defeat Satan entirely. Through Jesus' death, your body of sin was also brought to death so you are no longer enslaved to unrighteousness.[23] By becoming acquainted with the Holy Spirit, you have access to the same power that Jesus rose victorious with, and that power will begin to break generational curses from your life. It will take intentionality on your part, and many days will feel like a battle, but scripture says that where the Spirit of the Lord is, there is freedom.[24] You no longer have to carry the weight of your past on your shoulders. Release it to God, and watch His Spirit change you from the inside out.

Prepping for Purpose

Regardless of how you feel about yourself in this present moment, there is a completely different version of you that you have yet to meet. If you love yourself now, you will really love yourself once you begin walking in purpose. If you despise yourself now, just wait on who you will become once you give the Holy Spirit access to begin working inside of you.

If you believe that God is the creator of the universe, then you also believe He is the creator of purpose. Solomon says in Ecclesiastes that the whole duty of man is to fear God and keep His commandments.[25] Reverence and obedience are at the core of our worship to bring God glory. However, the vehicles that each person uses to achieve this goal will be different. Just as the sun has a different role than a tree, your purpose differs from everyone else's.

The temptation is to lock in on someone else's grind that you begin to curate your life to match theirs, but God was not selfish when He created you; He did not call you to share a lane with someone else. It is quite the opposite. The path that was paved for you can only be walked by you.

Your feet are the only ones graceful enough not to tire yet heavy enough to make an unforgettable impact. Crossing over into someone else's lane means there is an empty path not being walked with countless people left untouched. Because purpose is so specific, the only way you will fully find it is to let the Holy Spirit show you. In John 15, Jesus says that we can do nothing apart from Him.

To come out of the closet with boldness and confidence, you will need a game plan so that you don't go back. The following chapters will give practical advice on how to flee temptation and run toward holiness, but the key is to remember who is actually doing the work so that you don't fall into a pit of self-righteousness. The Holy Spirit is the true converter of human hearts. He does not act by force or deprivation but leaves it open for you to decide. I have not had an inkling of an attraction for another woman in years, not because I set a goal and stuck with it. I am changed because I chose to partner with the One who actually does the changing. There is no better partnership than becoming one with the Holy Spirit. He's got you.

CHAPTER VIII

Winning in the Wilderness

I INTRODUCE TO SOME and present to others one of the most legendary Pixar superheroes ever created—Violet Parr. If that name doesn't ring a bell, stop reading right now and watch *The Incredibles* and *The Incredibles 2*. Those movies will change your life. Those who have watched more than likely share common sentiments with me of nostalgia and childlike joy. Because I was the youngest of two, my brother was inherently the king of the remote control, so I rarely had a say on the types of movies we watched. *The Incredibles* was one that I enjoyed just as much as him because there were two sheroes in almost every frame: Violet and Elastigirl. Each time we watched that movie, we would pick which character we were, and I would always pick "Vi."

I was half of Violet's age when *The Incredibles* was first released in 2004, so she was close enough to my age for relatability yet old enough to admire. Violet Parr was a 14-year-old daughter of two superhero parents accompanied by two little brothers with their own special gifts. She swooned over Tony Rydinger but could never find the confidence to be herself when she talked to him. Granted, she was a superhero, so it was kind of her job to conceal that part of life and try to have a normal life with friends and engage in high-school drama like other girls her age. I won't spoil the movie, but there may have been a scene where Tony caught her in action, and he may or may not have lost his mind because of it. Even if you don't watch the entire movie, a quick YouTube search of this scene is comedic gold.

When Violet was out of Tony's sight, her insecurities went away and she became a bad-to-the-bone, self-assured, dangerous protector of the land as she fought off evil villains left and right. She had two superpowers that worked together to create an illusion that frustrated and eventually defeated her opponents. Violet possessed invisibility and the manipulation of force fields.

Without conducting statistical research on this, I am almost positive that invisibility is one of the top wished-for superpowers of the general population. Who doesn't want the ability to scare the living daylights out of people by becoming the ultimate prankster? I'd use my invisibility to walk through walls and never stand in a food line again. It's truly the ultimate hack that would make my life much more convenient. Invisibility was great for Violet until it wasn't. Any additional clothing or outside element applied to her body, with the exception of Edna's masterful Incredible costume, would reveal her whereabouts. Thus, her opponents would use a fire extinguisher or watch her footprints on the ground to locate her during battles. Violet's presence was only made known when she collided with an earthly element. I wouldn't go so far as to say her surroundings contributed to her weakness, but those external elements definitely attracted more heat from her opponents than if they were not there.

Though not as cool as invisibility but equally beneficial, Violet's second superpower was the manipulation of force fields. She could mentally generate an indestructible field that served as protection for herself and others. Violet's purple field was impenetrable to any outside force, and all who were inside of this field were safe. There is a scene where the whole Incredible gang was in the bounds of Violet's force field, rendering the opponent powerless. I don't know about you but if I was up against a bad guy, I would want Violet Parr on my team or at least a close equivalent.

Although we don't have to worry about colossal robots shooting lasers at us in a parking lot, we do have a lurking enemy on the prowl to take us out. In the world of sexuality and lust, the war is waged even more against those with a desire to be pure. It is not accidental that your particular weakness is dangled in front of you at the most inopportune times, and the more you say you're done with a certain person or situation, it becomes harder to walk away. Once you have finally decided to leave shame and guilt in the place that you found them and are ready to live a life of freedom, you are basically looking Satan in the eyes and saying, "Game on." You may not have the Incredibles at your defense, but the Holy Spirit has supernatural abilities that ensure your safety while you navigate uncharted territory. When you invite the Holy Spirit into your heart, the presence of God is a literal force field that covers you wherever you go. No longer are you bound by the limits of your fleshly endurance. Because Jesus is the image of the invisible God, the spirit that empowered Him will also grant you that same power if you choose to follow.

In Matthew 3 and 4, we read that Jesus encountered His own vulnerable moment after being baptized and receiving the Holy Spirit. As soon as He emerged from the water, heaven opened, and the Spirit of God descended like a dove to rest on Him. God then spoke publicly, declaring Jesus as beloved and pleasing to Him. This captured one of the most intimate scenes in the Bible where God the Father, the Son, and the Holy Spirit came together as one on Earth. I would think that called for a celebration, but Matthew's next mention is of Jesus being led into the wilderness. A bit untrusting of Matthew's sequence of events, I decided to see what Mark and Luke witnessed immediately following Jesus' baptism. Read their accounts below.

> "Then Jesus was led by the Spirit into the wilderness to be
> tempted by the devil."
> (MATTHEW 4:1 ESV)

"And a voice came from heaven, 'You are my beloved Son; with
you I am well pleased.' The Spirit immediately drove him out
into the wilderness. And he was in the wilderness forty days,
being tempted by Satan."
(MARK 1:11-12 ESV)

"And Jesus, full of the Holy Spirit, returned from the Jordan
and was led by the Spirit in the wilderness for forty days, being
tempted by the devil."
(LUKE 4:1-2 ESV)

Either all three New Testament writers conspired to throw us off or Jesus actually went to the wilderness immediately after His baptism. Under the assumption that this is true, not only did Jesus go into the darkness but He was driven there by this new Spirit in Him. I mean, He just received the Holy Spirit, and the first place they journeyed was to the middle of nowhere.

I have been in church all of my life, and nearly all of the sermons I heard on receiving the Holy Spirit were positive, life-giving messages promising a future full of hope and peaceful days. We are made alive with the Holy Spirit and none of the good He brings should be negated, but there is also a harsh reality often overlooked. Whether we choose to be in relationship with God, suffering will happen. Life with Christ is *not* an absence of pain, hardships, suicidal thoughts, lust-free relationships, or crushed dreams. Solomon says in Ecclesiastes 9:11 that time and chance happen to them all. If Jesus had to face temptation while being fully man and fully God, then you and I will have to face the enemy as well.

Though doubts will come, God absolutely knows what is best for us. There is purpose in our suffering, and there is a prize waiting for those who fight off Satan's tactics with discipline and self-control.[26] The purpose of your suffering is different from mine, but what is true is that nothing in this life is wasted. Temptation and darkness are out of your control, but you can make sure your team is stacked with the best defense to secure your victory.

The 3 Rs to Wage War With the Enemy

In the same way Satan studies you, you should also anticipate his attacks. The best way to know how and when the enemy is coming is to first know yourself. It is pointless to try to convince yourself that you are not attracted to the same sex if you know you are. I avoided the much-needed conversation with myself for years, hoping if I ignored it long enough that it would just go away. Truth is, you must iron out the wrinkles in your identity before you wear it out in public. People will only receive what you give so it's best to figure out who you are, what you like, and how you are lured to temptation before you step out of the closet and into the world.

Ultimately, a premeditated plan is needed whenever the enemy chooses to strike. In Matthew 4, Jesus is tempted on three separate occasions and offered a quick fix to ease His longings. Satan plays dirty that way. He hits us lightly enough to keep us alive but strong enough to make us suffer. The way that Jesus overcame temptation in the wilderness is our playbook for winning the war against the enemy every time. With a simple three-step process, I have fought my way out of dark moments several times over. Once this process becomes a discipline, you will spend less energy swinging at the enemy, and it will become second nature, like a reflex, to swat him away. In the wilderness, we see that Jesus resisted what was offered, recalled what was true, and repeated the process until Satan fled.

Resist

Hunger is an indicator of an unmet need, and it makes us painfully aware of the depraved nature of humanity. Think back to the garden of

Eden. Sin entered the world through the act of eating a piece of fruit. Adam and Eve ate the fruit and though it was enjoyable at the time, it brought forth ongoing disunion between man and God. Before the fall of man, Adam and Eve ate out of pleasure and abundance, not because they needed it to survive. Read the words God said to Adam before they were exiled from Eden:

> "Because you have listened to the voice of your wife and have
> eaten of the tree of which I commanded you, 'You shall not
> eat of it,' cursed is the ground because of you; and in pain you
> shall eat of it all the days of your life; thorns and thistles it shall
> bring forth for you; and you shall eat the plants of the field. By
> the sweat of your face you shall eat bread, till you return to the
> ground, for out of it you were taken.'"
> (Genesis 3:17-19 ESV)

Food, like most things in life, is only enjoyable to a certain point. If you don't believe me, try not to eat when you are hungry and take one more bite when you are stuffed. An insufficient amount of food will leave you angry and malnourished and too much of the wrong foods can lead to sickness, high blood pressure, and a lifelong journey of self-criticism. Managing a healthy and balanced diet is hard work and sometimes feels more painful than enjoyable. If nothing else, eating reminds us that we are deeply reliant on what is external because we cannot survive without it.

Furthermore, hunger is a form of desperation. When you become desperate enough, you will eat anything, and Satan knows that. In Matthew 4:2-3, Jesus had been fasting for 40 days and 40 nights. He was hungry, and Satan presented Him with an opportunity to eat. It seems ironic that Satan appeared to Jesus in a similar way to his appearance with Adam, but not really. Satan is as predictable as they come. His primetime moment is cued when you are weak, needy, or vulnerable. You can almost always expect Satan to occupy your places of discontentment with a dare, not a promise.

Satan said to Jesus, "If you are the Son of God, command these stones to become loaves of bread."[27] Here, Satan presents Jesus with a challenge to prove Himself by satisfying his own needs. The enemy will never be able to give you anything that you do not already have or to which you have access. Only God can supply all of your needs according to *His* riches and glory and because Satan is ill-equipped to perform Godly duties, he can only tempt you to perform in ways that were never meant for you.[28] Satan's dares come by whispers that sound like, "If you are _____, then _____". The word that fills the first blank represents the person you think you are, the person you want to be, or the person you've become. The second word is a challenge for you to prove that you are who you say you are. I'll share an example from my own life.

My personal wilderness is the land of inadequacy. I find myself stranded in this place often, especially when I don't have constant external affirmation from others. Satan knows I have wandered to this place long before I realized it, and he presents me with a challenge to prove that I actually don't belong there and that I'm adequate. He riddles me with dares like these:

If you are enough, do more.

If you are worthy, why are you still single?

If you are victorious over lust, why do you still struggle to abstain from it?

Every time he dares me, I am tempted to prove him wrong by setting a new goal, downloading another dating app, or uploading a new selfie or reel just to receive a few likes that will temporarily satisfy my longings. It took me a long time to realize that the enemy can persuade me to chase noble pursuits, and it can feel like it's from God. I'll say that one more time for you: The enemy can persuade you to chase noble pursuits, and it can feel like it's from God. However, David says in Psalm 33:20 (ESV), "Our soul waits for the Lord; he is our help and our shield." When in doubt, I know that unless I am led to the Lord to fulfill my longings, then it is highly possible that the enemy is at work. I now know that Satan is found in instant gratification, but God's power rests on those who wait for Him.

When I look at Jesus' example in His own wilderness, He resisted the challenge. Jesus did not perform the dance Satan dared him to do by turning the stones into bread. In fact, he was very familiar with what God could do in the wilderness based on what had already happened when the Israelites were hungry in the wilderness. In Exodus 16, God rained down "manna" from heaven to provide for the exiled people of Israel. Exodus 16:35 (ESV) says, "The people of Israel ate the manna for forty years, till they came to habitable land." Jesus could resist the immediate temptation because of his familiarity with the God who provides, sustains, and fulfills. Jesus resisted temptation because He knew the wilderness was only temporary and that God would see Him back to the land of abundance if only He waited for Him.

The same is true for you. You can resist the temptation to revisit old places and sleep with old people. You can deny the challenge to prove yourself when you know who you are. You can oppose the opposition when you realize you are on the winning team. Satan sings a different song to each of us, but it's the same old tune he used back in the garden of Eden. Follow Jesus' lead in the way He chose to wait on God. And when you're feeling weak, hold tight to 1 John 4:4 (ESV). It reads, "Little children, you are from God and have overcome them, for he who is in you is greater than he who is in the world."

Recall

Your journey of healing and path to freedom has less to do with acquiring more knowledge and more to do with utilizing the knowledge you already have. Even if you have never read the Bible a day in your life, you can use the pieces of scripture I have shared with you thus far as foundational blocks to build upon. Think of the areas you are most curious about and start there. From the first day I took interest in reading the Bible, I Googled the exact question that perplexed me. Millions of results flooded my search engine. I have no shame in going to Google rather than digging through a physical encyclopedia. I also have zero embarrassment from saying "I have no clue what any of this means." Matthew 7:7 (NLT) says, "Keep on seeking, and you will find."

One of the most exciting parts of walking with Jesus is the part where He gives us knowledge, little by little, each day. In John 15, Jesus tells us to abide in Him to bear much fruit.[29] Sometimes, I want to skip the abiding part and gather all the fruit to last me so I won't have to bother Him again, but that is so far from what He wants for me. God constantly reminds me that self-reliance is regressive to my faith whereas dependence upon Him signifies true growth. Believe it or not, the longer we stay the course, we progress back to childlike faith. We should be so needy of God that we want for nothing from the world. Besides, Satan cannot tempt us with something that we have resolved we do not need.

Each time Satan approached Jesus in the wilderness, he presented Jesus with an opportunity to show off His divinity. The first challenge was for Jesus to turn stones into bread. The second dare was for Jesus to throw Himself off a building so that the angels would catch him mid-air. Satan's final demand was for Jesus to bow down and worship him. This story can be viewed from various perspectives, but the one I find most helpful is for us to set our focus on the true intention of the enemy and how Jesus responds each time. With every new challenge, Satan gets closer to what he really wants from Jesus: Worship. Satan tempting Jesus to rearrange the elements of rocks to create bread can seem like he was genuinely concerned about Jesus' hunger. He wanted him fed, right? Why is that a bad thing? Well, he always starts his deceptive tricks with an unmet need, but he doesn't stop there.

Think of the last time you were lonely and a particular person or substance you've been staying away from grazed through your thoughts. Soon after, a catchy, familiar tune sang these words:

One time won't hurt. No one will know.
This will be the last time. For real this time.
Remember how good it feels?

At that moment, it becomes very difficult not to succumb to the dare unless you remember key promises from God to regain control of the situation. Recall Jesus' final words in Matthew 28:20 (ESV): "I am with you always, to the ends of the age" or Joshua 1:9 (ESV), "Do not be frightened, and do not be dismayed, for the Lord your God is with you wherever you go." That's not to say you'll immediately stop feeling lonely, but once you remember that you are always in the Father's company, Satan's words lose their tempting power.

As if preying on your weak spots is not enough, Satan then goes straight for the jugular by tempting you to harm yourself. I've had moments of suicidal thoughts. Maybe you have, too, but that is not the only way we are lured into self-harmful tactics. In a very physical way, Satan does not want us to be healthy, be it through unhealthy eating, abuse of alcohol and social drinking, or fiddling with perversion through pornography, premarital sex, and masturbation. Any area of your life without biblical conviction, accountability, and strict discipline can easily fall into the category of self-destruction. And though Satan will boastfully lead you to those dark places, he will not be there to clean up the debris after the storm. As a matter of fact, he won't admit to his actions. Instead, he will cast the blame on you which will lead you to further harm with another layer of self-pity, loathing, and guilt. He is not nice.

Before Satan gets a foothold, start speaking the Living Word of God over your life and into your life. Recall these truths:

"I am deeply loved by my Heavenly Father."
(ISAIAH 43:4; ROMANS 9:38-39)

"I was chosen to be here."
(EPHESIANS 1:4; JOHN 15:16)

"I am worthy enough for someone to die for me."
(JOHN 3:16; 1 CORINTHIANS 15:3)

"I am strong enough to get through this."
(2 CORINTHIANS 12:10; PSALM 29:11; PSALM 18:1-2)

"There is a purpose for my life."
(EPHESIANS 2:10; JEREMIAH 29:11; ROMANS 10:14-15)

"I am part of a community that needs me here."
(1 CORINTHIANS 12:26-27; ROMANS 12:4; MATTHEW 18:20)

"I am waiting for God's best for me."
(ISAIAH 40:31; 2 CORINTHIANS 4:17-18)

"My desires are heard by the One who can meet them."
(PSALM 37:4, MATTHEW 6:11, MATTHEW 7:11)

"My body is a temple, and it carries a treasure."
(1 CORINTHIANS 6:19-20; 2 CORINTHIANS 4:7)

Last but certainly not least, Satan is bloodthirsty for your worship. After being exiled from heaven, he needs you to glorify him and he wants nothing more than to take God's place in your life, but know that he only has power if you forget the Source of your own. Hebrews 4:12 (ESV) proclaims:

> For the word of God is living and active, sharper than any two-edged sword, piercing to the division of soul and of spirit, of joints and marrow, and discerning the thoughts and intentions of the heart.

The enemy cowers at the Sword of Scripture; therefore, you must never forget to carry it wherever you go.

As hungry as Jesus was in the wilderness, He managed to say, "Man shall not live by bread alone, but by every word that comes from the mouth of God."[30] So, you can say I shall not be controlled by my physical nature. I will not give my body to anyone who God hasn't given them permission to have. I will not live for the validation of another person, *but by every word that comes from the mouth of God.*

Repeat

Why would Satan distort God's original commandment to Eve and relay the wrong message to Adam? Why does he constantly question the identity of Christ through all of scripture, while nature points us to who He truly is? What reason would justify why Jesus had to tell Satan "no" three times for him to finally receive the message?

I have resolved that Satan has difficulty hearing or he wants to make sure we mean what we say. Matthew 4 shows Jesus resisting temptation and speaking truth repeatedly. He was consistent in his objections, and he refused to be tricked and distracted. If nothing else, Jesus was unwavering, adamant, and prepared. He was well aware of himself, the situation, his surroundings, and the end goal which was to exit the wilderness victorious.

Consistency means to be in agreement with something; to remain in harmony. Jesus was on one accord with the Holy Spirit inside of Him and in alignment with God who was watching over Him. James calls for us to resist the devil so he will flee, and this is not a one-time deal.[31] James is prompting us to act in a repetitive manner; that is, to form a lifestyle of righteousness.

The truth of the matter is that Satan is dead set on taking you out by destroying you or altering the original plan for your life. Think about it this way: Had Jesus only had one scripture memorized, He would have been ill-equipped the next time. Denying the first drink may not be enough. Scrolling past an old text thread once won't get the job done.

Convincing yourself that this time is the last time will not end in victory. Jesus' example for winning in the wilderness was to make a practice of living for righteousness. To live a life free from Satan is to make a habit of telling him no while basking in the promises of God. Discernment is much easier once you have the truth living inside of you. Spiritual maturity does not come with age but with time spent in the presence of God.

Michael Jordan set the standard for many men for dunking a basketball. The way he weaved a ball between his legs and soared in the air like an eagle led hundreds of thousands of men to attempt to mimic everything he did. Jordan was and is an icon. The poster for the Christian, however, is Jesus. The way we study His actions and tattoo His words on our bodies signify that He is our icon, but looking the part is not enough. It's actually more embarrassing than a person with all the right sports gear that cannot make the sports team. 2 Timothy 2:15 advises us to make every effort to present ourselves approved and acceptable to God. We don't just spit out random, out-of-context verses and do Christian things, but we actually study the actions, intentions, and heart of Christ. Even still, the standard is great, and we will fall short.

Our journey through the wilderness will sometimes break us down to pieces. We will give in, say yes, and fail again but we have three superheroes at our defense—God, the Father, looking over us and going before us; Jesus, the Son, pleading for grace to be flooded upon us each time we fail; and the Holy Spirit who empowers us from the inside as He helps us to preserve to the end. The journey will look different for each of us, but the good news is that victory has already been secured. The only question left is will you choose the winning team?

Chapter IX

Coming Out

THE YEAR 2020 WAS A TIME OF collective isolation. No one chose solitary confinement, but it was forced upon us. Within the bounds of our homes, apartments, and dorm rooms, we had to finally slow down and face ourselves. Our comforts, dare I say distractions, were restricted due to social distancing, masking, and curfews. The mindless scroll through social media apps were not so mindless anymore as timelines were infiltrated with opinions on racial issues, the pending election, and natural disasters. We needed each other, but the circumstances that surrounded us caused a division that made it impossible to be together. On the largest scale possible, our entire world was in a helpless state.

In the same way that fear of the unknown kept thousands of people from going outside for over a year, I hid in the bounds of my closet space for even longer. The shame of my past and the guilt from those I had hurt along the way prevented me from breaking free. I was afraid of unmasking and infecting others with my brokenness. It wasn't until I listened to a sermon by Pastor Sarah Jakes Roberts in 2019 that forced me to entertain the thought of my life being meant for more. Though skeptical at first, I started to consider how life would be if I began living on the other side of my doubts and fears. What if I had an essential role to contribute to the world's disease-stricken state of sin? Could I make it less scary for others who experienced something similar? I prayed that God would begin to show me the calling for my life and build the character I needed for me to fully walk it out.

Maybe you have also wasted a considerable amount of time waiting for someone to rescue you from your closet space and forgot that you hold the key to let yourself out. Perhaps you simply needed a reminder that God has gone to great lengths to reconcile your relationship with Him by providing the cure to this spiritual pandemic of sin through the crucifixion and resurrection of Jesus Christ. It is no longer a question of whether a sinner can have a relationship with a holy, impartial God. Rather, the question is do they want to have a relationship? The walls between you and your future do not need a demolition team and a clean-up crew. There is a door for you to walk through and it can only be opened by you. No matter how badly I want you to be free of the confinements of darkness, I cannot drag you out of it by force.

As we are coming to an end, I must leave the decision to you as I also had to decide who I would be once I came out and what I would leave behind. I am well aware that my story is not everyone's and that my job is not to make everyone like me. You are on your journey to figuring it all out, and there is a huge chunk of people that won't walk with Jesus by the end of this book, and I understand that.

At the very least, I hope I brought clarity to your situation and gave you an ounce of hope on your journey thus far. I hope I have been the friend that has shown empathy and helped you sort through difficult emotions. I hope you felt my arms extending to you through my story, assuring you there are better days ahead. In vulnerability, I have shared pieces of my life with you to shed light on the agony that pains many individuals who have encountered same-sex attraction and felt isolated from Christian communities because of it. If I have rattled parts within your soul that feel convicting and uncomfortable, it was not my intention, but I would have done a huge disservice by not introducing or re-introducing the Gospel of Jesus Christ. The God who has captured my heart and graced me with freedom and unspeakable joy wants to provide you that same opportunity. My high school love story was special, and it has undoubtedly propelled me into my purpose, but God's relentless pursuit of my heart is the greater love story, and He is the only reason I am still here. I want nothing more than for you to experience Him similarly. Whether you choose a relationship with God, I know that humans were made for each other, and the journey that is meant for you to embark on cannot be walked alone. So, whether it is Jesus, Tom, or Jane, there must be someone you let in to help guide you out. A relationship requires a compromise from both parties. I'm not sure about Tom or Jane, but Jesus is always on one knee offering a box of abundant life to you. Scripture has proven Christ's love by the sacrifices and compromises He has already made. To respond to what He has done, hence the Gospel, you now have to make compromises to live in this relationship with Him. Jesus asking to spend an eternity with you is a lot to consider, and you should really search your heart before you respond because you only have two choices: *Yes, Jesus, I am choosing You,* or *No, Jesus, I am choosing to do life without You.*

Both choices have eternal consequences and there is no right or wrong answer. Yes, I am a Christian confirming that whatever choice you choose is up to you because you are the one who has to live with it. I am not the determinant of right or wrong nor do I desire that role. My only job is to introduce you to the One who has proven true to me, to encourage you throughout your process, and to love you regardless of the choice you make. I must forewarn you, though, that time is of the essence. Every breath we breathe is a gift, and the next moment is not promised. In a sense, you have the rest of your life to accept Jesus' proposal but in a sobering and real way, the choice you make right now could potentially be your last opportunity to lock in what you truly want.

For three years, I was given the opportunity to choose Jesus every Sunday morning at church and every Tuesday night during college ministry. It wasn't until my final semester of nursing that I decided to recommit my life to Jesus and make the necessary compromises to secure my eternity with God. Since my high school relationship, I had entertained two other women romantically in college and both ended in betrayal. I also talked to guys and those situations were far from perfect as well. No matter how many times I prayed that those relationships would work out, they only got worse, and I eventually found myself alone yet again. Throughout each relationship, which was usually between six and 12 months, I would go that long without being in communion with God. I slowly began to realize that sin not only kills but also separates. I knew what it felt like to pray and hear God respond, but something about what I was doing and how I was living estranged me from His presence, leaving a hollow sense of loneliness that no companion could soothe. Depression does not come close to describing the depths of darkness that encompassed me during those six-to-12-month stints. Sin was keeping me from experiencing the fullness of God's love which also separated me from the purpose He had created within me. After several bouts of suicidal ideation and two close attempts to act on those thoughts, I decided to finally say yes to Jesus.

My decision to walk away from this lifestyle was a hard and grueling process, especially since I walked through it alone for the most part. The church communities were still not talking about same-sex struggles, and I was petrified of how they would view me if I exposed all of my rainbow skeletons. Instead, I spent most days journaling out my most vulnerable emotions and raw desires to God. He knew everything I felt anyway, but it was important for me to cry my heart out to Him. God's love holds a special space for our ugliest parts with no judgment. With time, I realized my heart had always belonged to God, but I continued to give it away because I didn't trust that He could tend to it well. I let the enemy convince me that He didn't create it right to begin with which led me to seek validation and approval from other people. I was oblivious to the fact that each relationship was a way for me to prove that I deserved to be here and that I was worthy of love because I never believed I was worthy at all. It is quite enlightening to see all that is crouched in the darkness once you allow the light of Jesus inside.

A year had passed since I had been romantically involved with anyone, and I would be lying to say that the thought of going back had not crossed my mind. In vulnerable moments, my mind naturally reverted to the comforts I once ran to when I was vulnerable. On top of fighting my thoughts, I also had to constantly look away from a society that had become more accepting than ever of sexual fluidity. Television shows, social media, and church pulpits were beginning to preach that it's okay to love who you want and be whoever you want, showing a blatant disregard for God as the Creator of the universe with a purpose and plan for each of His creations. Moreover, my decision to walk away from same-sex attraction led to me ending key friendships that I had spent an immeasurable amount of time investing in. I tried my best to at least retain cordiality with my previous romantic partners by setting boundaries. It can be done, but it did not work for me. I completely lost those relationships and that was a hard reality to face, but the compromise I was required to make to live in constant unity with God was to hate sin in the same manner He did which sometimes means creating distance from the person who tempts you to sin. Be that as it may, I was not completely sold on the fact that the mere act of being sexually attracted to the same sex was a sin, so I needed to investigate the exact sin I was learning to hate. 1 John 3:9-10 was a scripture I stumbled upon that propelled me to ask more questions:

> No one born of God makes a practice of sinning, for God's seed abides in him; and he cannot keep on sinning, because he has been born of God. By this it is evident who are the children of God, and who are the children of the devil: whoever does not practice righteousness is not of God, nor is the one who does not love his brother.[32]

John was very clear about one thing: If I am born of God, that is, of God's people, it is impossible to continue living in sin. That passage further confirmed that living in sin was wrong, but I needed a firmer conviction to solidify the decision I was choosing. Once again, I had to fall back on the adamant Word of God because every other source was too shaky. Since the Bible is filled with do's, don'ts, and a lot of gray, I kept it simple and went back to the Ten Commandments.

God spoke these commandments to the Israelites on Mount Sinai immediately after He brought them from Egypt declaring them His people and He their God. Since they were God's people, it was appropriate for Him to give them conditions by which to live. Likewise, if I have been born of God and declared His people then I also have conditions by which to live. The first commandment God gave them, and the holy grail of the Christian faith, is to not create other gods before Him.[33] In modern times, I wouldn't typically build a golden sculpture to fall down and worship like the Israelites. I love cars, clothes, and nice houses which are easy for me to worship, but more than that, a person made in the likeness of God proved far more attractive than anything else, especially when God was not sitting on the throne of my heart.

When I looked back on each relationship, I undeniably worshipped the ground that each of those people walked on, so much so that I had no room for anyone else. I barely prayed because I was too busy making my requests known to them. I didn't read my Bible because I held close to the words of the future that we promised ourselves. A clear sign of my idolization of those women, above all else, was that I was claiming ownership of them as if they were mine and I was theirs. Exodus 20:5 (NLT) says, "You must not bow down to worship them, for I, the Lord your God, am a jealous God who will not tolerate your affection for any other gods."

Those words barked at me then and have rung in my ears and echoed in my heart ever since. Though those verses are not as specific to same-sex attraction as other passages of scripture, those were the words God spoke to me that sealed my faith in Christ. Those people's brokenness could never mend my brokenness; their pain only bled into my pain; they needed God just as much as I did. I was an unfit god for them, and they could never take the place of God for me.

It has been four years since I recommitted my life to Jesus, and I can honestly say I am not triggered as often as I was. I know my weaknesses and the places I need to avoid to honor my commitment to the Lord. I don't want to cheat on God any more than I want someone else to cheat on me. The only part I wish I could change about everything that happened is the memories that sneak up on me at the most inconvenient times. The enemy still tries to take advantage of those vulnerable moments by luring me back into the closet to wallow in the shame of my past. With time, though, he has become surprisingly easier to identify and dismiss. Through prayer, devotion, and a healthy support system, I am constantly reminded that God's presence is a place of safety and freedom.

In the last chapter, we added the 3 Rs to our playbook to resist the temptation of Satan, but no one wins a game without points on the board. To truly secure your victory, you will need an offensive plan which will cause you to take a leap of faith outside of the corridors of your closet. If your heart is saying, *"Yes, Lord, I am choosing You,"* then you are ready to compromise how you choose to live your life today to take hold of what lies ahead. It is time to unlock the door and live OUT your faith. That's right: O-U-T, OUT. O stands for **O**wn your truth, U is to **U**tilize the church, and T is to **T**ry therapy.

Own Your Truth

By this point of the process, I imagine you doing a *should I or should I not* dance with your doorknob, agonizing over the list of pros and cons to freedom. There is safety in holding a secret that no one knows, but the byproduct of hiding from those who hurt you is isolation from those who can aid in your healing. I used to live by the quote, "What they don't know won't hurt them" until I experienced oblivion firsthand from someone who had been disloyal to me for several months without my knowledge. Withholding information only prolongs the actual hurt that someone would feel once they are made aware of the secret, but more than that, it is hardly about the person you are trying to protect and all about how that secret affects you. Are you afraid of what they would think of you or are you afraid of how their opinions would make you feel? Is it the fear of walking by faith or is it the possibility of losing certain people that may not have access to the journey God is taking you on? What if *this* is your moment to take full advantage of the momentum rising inside of you to finally release the weight of shame that has burdened you for so long, even if it means doing something you have never done before? What would hold you back?

I was teetering on the fence between hot and cold for an extensive amount of time during my first few years of following Christ. I wanted to be friends with Jesus while taking full advantage of what the world had to offer, and it was all in the name of being a light to the lost world. Matthew 5:16 (KJV) says, "Let your light so shine before men, that they may see your good works, and glorify your Father which is in heaven." This is a great verse but when given out of context, it is dan-ger-ous.

Earlier in the passage, Jesus says a city on a hill cannot be hidden which implies that our light should shine from the hill that is set apart from the plains and valleys around us. By no means are we encouraged to sift through the valleys of sin hoping that our light will put out another's darkness. When we pretend to be the source of light to those around us, it may lead to our souls being snatched in the process. Only Jesus can transform someone's heart because He is the light. Your job as a Christ-follower is to own the light inside of you by allowing it to shine through you.

Owning the light inside of you is the single greatest gift you can give to yourself and the world. From a faith-based perspective, we are not given much in this world to call our own. Every good and perfect gift comes from God and is a demonstration of His grace. Our homes, cars, children, businesses, friends, and investment plans are nice and all, but we cannot truly say we would have in it our possession unless the good Lord decided it beforehand. Peter instructs us to cherish each of our gifts by serving others as good stewards of God's grace.[34] In other words, we were loaned nice things to give nice things. The one gift you were given complete dominion to rule and control is yourself, meaning you are fully responsible for your property and yours only. Your partner will not be held responsible for your grass not being cut, your roof caving in, or the moldy walls separating you from the outside world. While it is true that she may have contributed to your poor living conditions, she will not have to stand before the Builder of the property and defend it on the day of foreclosure. Although there will be a righteous lawyer that stands between you and the Judge, making a case for your innocence, you hold all of the power today to renovate yourself to be someone you are proud to show off. Besides, we love a good side-by-side before-and-after picture.

I am choosing to use the homeownership metaphor because I want you to see yourself as invaluable as a multi-million-dollar mansion. The raw and broken parts of you are necessary pieces of the grander version that is to come, and though the mansion is not fully built, its value does not change. Trust the Great Architect's blueprint of how the building process will go. Embrace the days when you are filthy with dirt, knowing the end-product will be refined and polished. Rainy days may slow down the process, but the sun will soon shine again. So, dance in the rain and get comfortable with the mud because you will need to remember your worst days to appreciate your best ones ahead.

Your truth is simply embracing who you are today in light of who you were yesterday with all of the hopes and fears of becoming who you will be tomorrow. You've done things you are not proud of, and things have been done to you that you had no control over. You don't know everything there is to know because you were never meant to find out some things. Call out the parts of you due for updates and choose not to return to the outdated version, even when it's familiar. Remove people from your life who refuse to value the worth that Jesus died to give you. Admit the weak points of your faith and replace them with the immovable promises of God. Above all else, waste not another of life's precious moments fearing what could happen. Instead, walk into every day as the sole person who can contribute to what you want to come to pass.

Utilize the Church

Because Jesus is not physically bent down in a bodily stature before you, you may find yourself questioning the legitimacy of this alleged relationship He wants with you. The uniqueness of your encounter with Jesus will be different than mine but it makes His invitation no less real. There is a divine tangibility that breaks through the carnal nature of your being when the Spirit of God chooses to have a private meeting with you and only you. Once you open the door to your heart, the Spirit makes your soul His dwelling place, replacing your old heart of stone with a new heart of flesh. This spiritual shift occurring inside of you manifests in a very physical way, denying any opportunity for your imagination to take the credit. Sometimes, it can feel like butterflies in your stomach or a heatwave rushing over you. It is normal to feel a bit nervous with sweaty palms or like you can't sit still. Tears may trickle down your face in the absence of sadness and you may find yourself bowing to your knees in the absence of fatigue. God's love becomes undeniably palpable in those moments, especially once you remember your rebellion and undeservingness. Still, He meets you with gentleness rather than condemnation as He remembers the sacrifice that Christ already made on behalf of your past, present, and future sins. The reality of it all is so overwhelming that you cannot help but anticipate the next outpouring of His presence.

Supernatural encounters with God typically don't just happen, though. There must be a level of intentionality on your part along with a posture of worship. Worship is simply making space to give God's Word back to Him because you know He is worthy. I don't know about you, but it can get really hard to set my heart to worship at home when there's

Netflix, people talking on the phone, toddlers running around, and food waiting to be cooked. If you don't believe me, try worshiping God from underneath your weighted blanket. You'll wake up four hours later without a clue of the date let alone that you were intentionally setting the stage for an encounter with God. I am not saying you cannot experience God in your living room with the dishwasher going and your child tugging at your pant leg, but the level of intimacy you once experienced with Him alone would be very low if intimate at all. Remember that this is a relationship, and it takes two people pursuing one another for it to be sustained. God has never and will never stop flooding you with His love and devotion, but you cannot passively expect His love to maintain your affections.

If there has ever been a moment when you have felt a distance between you and God, rest assured that He is incapable of distancing His love from you. In Romans 8, Paul fervently declares:

> For I am sure that neither death nor life, nor angels nor rules, nor things present nor things to come, nor powers, nor height nor depth, nor anything else in all creation, will be able to separate us from the love of God in Christ Jesus our Lord.[35]

After being in grave isolation for so long, the fragility of your spiritual health will be at an all-time high because you are closer to your past than the future God prepared for you. Like a newborn's entrance into the world, you would benefit greatly from a tribe of people who are safe yet capable of nurturing your spiritual growth in Christ. They should also be just as desperate for an encounter with God as you are and committed to reminding you of His ongoing love for you. Joining a local church community may not have been at the top of your "freshly outside" to-do list, but it is imperative to not retreat to your past.

The church is the most intentional place for people to gather who have set their hearts to worship and are longing for a supernatural encounter with God. It is an integral part of the Christian's faith for the individual person and the collective body as a whole. Church for the individual is a place for anyone. Isaiah 55 reads, "Come, everyone who thirsts, come to the waters; and he who has no money, come, buy and eat! Come, buy wine and milk without money and without price."[36] It sounds chaotic and very well can be as many have experienced firsthand. The possibilities of someone being offended, judged, talked about, or shunned are endless since the invitation is open to anyone and it's free. If we compare the open-door experience of going to church for zero dollars to a free Beyonce concert, the mere difference is the likelihood of where God's presence will abide. To put it differently, which place would the transformative power of God most likely be in full effect? A place where people go to be entertained or a place for people preparing for their eternity? Church may be a come-all place for sinners and saints, but if it weren't, hardly any of us would actually meet the entrance requirements. Rather than minding the next person's business, church is much better when we focus on where our faith journey takes us and how God kneads the kinks out of our souls.

On the other hand, church for the collective congregation is multi-purposeful as we each have gifts and abilities that contribute to the greater mission of Christ. Before Jesus ascended to heaven, He gave His followers strict instructions to finish what He started. In this familiar charge, also known as the Great Commission, He states:

> Go therefore and make disciples of all nations, baptizing them in the name of the Father and of the Son and of the Holy Spirit, teaching them to observe all that I have commanded you. And behold, I am with you always, to the end of the age (Matthew 28: 19-20 ESV).

It is important to note that once you become one with Christ, you are no longer a victim of trauma in need of a rescuer. Your rescue has arrived, revived you back to life, and has welcomed you to the Land of the Living. That is, those who are spiritually alive. The collective purpose of the church is to introduce Jesus to spiritual zombies believing in full faith that He can bring them back to life, but the vehicles that it uses will be unique to the individual's talents that God has blessed them with. If anyone hides His gifts, the mission will be hindered because of it, as scripture states, "For the body does not consist of one member but many."[37]

Even if you are convinced that the church is a necessary aspect of your faith, finding one fit for you may not be an easy task. If you are wondering what to look for in a church and how to know if it is a safe place for you to join, know that the qualifiers for what makes a church worthy of nurturing your soul are subjective to you. When in doubt, I frequently refer to the first church of Christians in the book of Acts. Acts 2:42-47 (ESV) reads:

> And they devoted themselves to the apostles' teaching and the fellowship, to the breaking of bread and the prayers. And awe came upon every soul, and many wonders and signs were being done through the apostles. And all who believed were together and had all things in common. And they were selling their possessions and belongings and distributing the proceeds to all, as any had need. And day by day, attending the temple together and breaking bread in their homes, they received their food with glad and generous hearts, praising God and having favor with all the people. And the Lord added to their number day by day those who were being saved.

The congregation was devoted to one another. They enjoyed being together whether eating, serving, praying, or having yard sales. It did not matter what someone smelled like or who they were attracted to because everyone was focused on praising God. The small numbers did not affect their attitudes, either. When God felt it was time for an increase, He added more people to the patterns that they had already established. If you find a group of praying people who are generous, disassociated with gossip, and dead set on uplifting God's name, it wouldn't be a terrible idea to stay after church for free lunch to further investigate whether they are a good fit for you and vice versa.

I realize that many have been deeply wounded by the institution of the church, and you have already decided you will never return to its doors. I, like you, have been a victim of spiritual abuse and it takes time to heal before you can try again. All I am saying is to *try again*. I truly believe there is a congregation of saints waiting to welcome you with open arms, guiding you away from sinfulness while loving you through it. Most importantly, your purpose is attached to the body of Christ. You are the missing limb of someone's congregation that needs you to be you so that they will be more complete. Your gifts are necessary for the church to be fully operational. It needs you just as much as you need it.

Your faith journey may begin in solitude, but there is no way it can be sustained without actively loving a community of believers, receiving their love, and holding one another accountable. Jesus says in Matthew 22:36-40 (ESV):

> You shall love the Lord your God with all of your heart and with all your soul and with all your mind. This is the first and greatest commandment. And a second is like it: You shall love your neighbor as yourself.

When Jesus invites us into a relationship with Him, He doesn't give us an option to solo-dolo it the rest of the way, and coming from an introvert who struggles with being around people, that is a very good thing.

Try Therapy

If you are in the aforementioned group of individuals that have been beaten down spiritually, emotionally, or physically by the church or another religious affiliation, it will be nearly impossible to trust anyone again without working through your trauma. The atrocities inflicted upon you will require the attention of a professional with a special skill set to guide you on your path of healing. A doctor is an expert on the body, and a therapist is an expert of the mind. Both are essential if you are wounded. As a healthcare professional, I always recommend that my patients receive multiple opinions. One psychiatrist's reading of your results is their interpretation which should always be followed by a second or third opinion to fully trust the original diagnosis. Likewise, the first therapist may be unfit for your needs, but that is why God blessed us with thousands more. Here are five reasons why anyone can and should try therapy:

1. "When you are emotionally healthy, you are more powerful spiritually." – Dr. Anita Phillips
2. The worst-case scenario is that you don't find one and end up without a therapist again.
3. The best-case scenario is finding someone willing to be honest with you so that you can finally be honest with yourself.
4. A shift of perspective is necessary, especially when everyone around you believes the same thing.
5. If God cares about your entire well-being, you should, too.

CHAPTER X

The Story of Eternity

When you started this journey with me, I was 15 years old and had just found out that my best friend was romantically attracted to me. I didn't know what I thought about it at the time, but I did know I loved her and did not want to lose her. I had always been taught that the Bible was against homosexuality, so I instantly felt like I was doing something wrong before I did anything at all. I tried to sort it out by myself by ending our friendship, but that didn't work. It only made the relationship more intense and codependent. I reached a point where I was desperate for biblical counsel, and at the moment that I decided to share what I was going through at church, some kid in youth group made a careless remark about a gay person they knew. I shrank in fear, went into the closet, and hid underneath the blanket of shame for several years. God grew silent, and out of frustration, I hardened my heart toward Him and the church, deciding that they could no longer be trusted. You found me when I was clinging to fear and solitude as my ride or dies, because they were always waiting for me in the darkness whenever I felt small and worthless. I had resolved that God created me wrong, and that if I ever allowed people to really see who I was, they would agree.

I have not always acknowledged teenage Alexis. I have actually tried to keep her tucked away for a very long time, but for some reason, I could never put her to rest. Even after I found Christ, I did not understand why part of me felt locked away as if I wasn't truly free. Then, as plain as day, God showed me why. He said these words to me: "I cannot allow you to walk away from your closet for good without first bringing the rest of my children out with you."

You are part of my freedom.

You hold a large plot in my story.

You are the reason I fought tooth and nail with Satan and why I am dead set on staying the course.

Now that I have done my part to the best of my ability to safely guide you back to outside living, you are responsible for what comes next. The story of eternity has already been written and your name is in it. You were never meant to be stored away like an old trophy collecting dust just watching life pass. Rather, you were created on purpose for purpose. Hear me loud and clear: You were created *on* purpose *for* purpose and your purpose is hidden in your identity.

In God's kingdom, you are not defined by your sexual preferences nor are there distinctions in who you are. Galatians 3:28 (NIV) proclaims, "There is neither Jew or Greek, neither slave nor free, nor is there male or female, for you are all in Christ." Similarly, Romans 10:12-13 (NIV) confirms:

> For there is no difference between Jew and Gentile—the same Lord is Lord of all and richly blesses all who call on him, for, "Everyone who calls on the name of the Lord will be saved."

The only place where worldly attributes define you is in the world. As much as I appreciate the people within the LGBTQIA+ community, I refuse to lessen the value of my identity by defining myself by who I have been involved with. God doesn't see those letters when He looks at me, and He isn't calling you any of those names, either. When He looks at you, He sees Jesus or your sin, and since the world doesn't give us many options, I've made a simplified list of biblically-based identities that one will fall into. You are a creation of God, a creation of God and a child of

God or a creation of God, a child of God and one who is called by God. Let me explain.

Without any acknowledgment from anyone, every living being was first created by God. "In the beginning, God created the heavens and the earth" (Genesis 1:1 ESV). I love science nearly as much as I love scripture, and it has yet to be disproved that God created the entire universe. Whether a person wants anything to do with God is a different conversation, but it is an undeniable fact that we are all His creation.

The next category of being a child of God is strictly based on how a person responds to Christ. Jesus explains this in John 3 where He says:

> Truly, truly I say to you, unless one is born of water and the Spirit, he cannot enter the kingdom of God. That which is born of the flesh is flesh, and that which is born of the Spirit is spirit.[38]

In other words, you can live by and identify with the world's standards, rules, and labels or you can choose to be rebirthed by the Holy Spirit who gradually transforms you into a new creation. A child of God is not someone born into a Christian family, nor is it someone who just goes to church. Contrary to popular belief, a child of God is not a privilege either. John 1:12-13 (ESV) firmly states:

> But to all who did receive him [Jesus], who believed in his name, he gave the right to become children of God, who were born not of blood nor of the will of the flesh nor of the will of man, but of God.

A child of God is a right, granted by God, requiring a present relationship with Jesus Christ.

Last but not least, after you have been welcomed into the family of God, there is a specific calling only He can fulfill through you. God's calling is similar to a phone call where you are on the receiving end with the option to accept or decline. For many, God has been dialing your line nonstop with an urgent message to rid yourself of whatever distractions you have so you can finally hear what He has been trying to tell you. Maybe you have an idea of the gifts and talents you've been given or the general direction of where your life should go but if you want clarity to God's purpose for your life, it is time to stop avoiding His call.

You see, following Christ for salvation alone is not enough for the person who wants to win in the wilderness. Not going to hell is just that, but waging war with hell on Earth is a whole different ball game in which only a handful of game-changers are willing to participate. Game-changers only know how to compete, and they are strangers to playing it safe. You fit into this category if you recognize the calling in your life and the impact your life will have on the next person. You're the type of person with such a vengeance toward Satan's agenda that even if it costs your life, you are willing to lay it down going forward for the sake of the good news of Christ. God wants to shine His glorious light through you as one of His vessels. The world has yet to see all that God can do, and part of it is because His chosen vessels have been filled with shame, doubt, and fear, but today, I say no more.

Choose today to no longer hide underneath the clutter of your past. Allow this to be the moment where you wholeheartedly decide to seek a life that has been hidden with Christ in God.[39] Jesus did not fulfill God's plan for salvation by shrinking in fear. Instead, He exemplified how to be courageous in the face of fear. The presence of God upon your life is not designed to be shoved into a hole in the wall, but His presence is powerful enough to tear down a lifetime of walls that have been built. The closet is simply too small for the overflow of abundant life that God has waiting for you on the other side. You were meant for more so refuse to settle for less. If you're feeling pressured, don't. God is a good, good Father who will patiently guide you step-by-step, hand-in-hand, as He reveals His plan to you in gradual amounts. I know you feel ready to take it all by storm, but do not rush your process. In due time, God will make your crooked path straight as long as you stay the course.

So...

What do you think about all of that? What do you say to coming out with Jesus? I have done it already, and trust me when I say the vibes are *immaculate* from out here. If you're ready, too, here is how it is done:

First, open the door.
Second, take in the view of the Father's love outstretched to you.
Finally, run into His hands and vow to never look back.

***

You have been crouched in your closet, arms clenched around your knees with your face buried in your lap for so long... until a bright light beamed underneath your door alluring you to crack it open. You had to dig deep, but you eventually found your inner courage leading you to open the door. You danced around a bit but eventually grabbed the knob, and the door swung open. Here, you stand in your door frame, immediately captivated by the breeze of fresh air drying your tears before they fall. You close your eyes to breathe in the sweet fragrance of peony, immediately forgetting the reeking odor of your past. You lift your foot to take a step only to realize you are already in the air. A little uneasy, you squeeze your eyes even tighter, and panic rises within you. The heights of the unknown have never been your thing. Before your routine-spiraling episode goes into full throttle, a kind voice of assurance speaks to you from below. You slowly open your eyes to look down and see a fatherly being carrying you on His shoulders. He speaks a language only your soul can understand. While you try to make sense of what is actually happening, the wind picks up and you discover Him running with you into the field of your dreams. Your childhood fantasies, your million-dollar acting career, the family, and kids are all projected onto the yellow grains of wheat. A mixture of joy and sorrow sweeps over you as you reconnect with the grief of burying those dreams long ago while being amazed at their resurrection before you. The Man with a kind voice comes to an easy halt, looks up to you, and says, "Eyes have not seen, and ears have not heard, and no mind has imagined what I have prepared for you, my love."

NOTES

1 https://www.lexico.com/en/definition/shame

2 2 Timothy 2:15 ESV

3 Genesis 2:7 ESV

4 Pickett, Brent, "Homosexuality", *The Stanford Encyclopedia of Philosophy* (Spring 2021 Edition), Edward N. Zalta (ed.), forthcoming URL = <https://plato.stanford.edu/archives/spr2021/entries/homosexuality/>.

5 Guy M. Richard et al., "Where Did Satan Come from?" November 15, 2018, https://www.thegospelcoalition.org/article/satan-come-from/.

6 https://www.collinsdictionary.com/us/dictionary/english/deceit

7 "The Roles of the Woman and the Man in Genesis 3," accessed January 11, 2021, https://www.thegospelcoalition.org/themelios/article/the-roles-of-the-woman-and-the-man-in-genesis-3/.

8 Matthew Henry, "Matthew 22," Matthew 22 Matthew Henry's Commentary (Bible Hub), accessed January 16, 2021, https://biblehub.com/commentaries/mhc/matthew/22.htm.

9 Urban Dictionary https://www.urbandictionary.com/define.php?term=in%20the%20closet

10 Poythress, V. S. (2012). How Can Only One Religion Be Right? In Inerrancy and Worldview: Answering Modern Challenges to the Bible (p. 21). essay, Crossway.

11 John 1:4 ESV

12 Revelation 3:20 ESV

13 Romans 5:8 ESV; 2 Corinthians 5:17

14 Isaiah 55:11

15 John 10:1-13 NLT

16 Romans 5:7 ESV

17 https://williamsinstitute.law.ucla.edu/publications/conversion-therapy-and-lgbt-youth/

[18] https://familyproject.sfsu.edu/sites/default/files/FAP_Family%20Acceptance_JCAPN.pdf

[19] Hebrews 12:2

[20] 1 Peter 5:8 ESV

[21] 2 Corinthians 3:18 ESV

[22] 2 Corinthians 5:17 ESV

[23] Romans 6:6 ESV

[24] 2 Corinthians 3:17

[25] Ecclesiastes 12:13-14 ESV

[26] 1 Corinthians 9:24-27

[27] Matthew 4:3 ESV

[28] Philippians 4:19 ESV

[29] John 15:4 ESV

[30] Matthew 4:4 ESV

[31] James 4:7 ESV

[32] 1 John 3:9-10 ESV

[33] Exodus 20:3 ESV

[34] 1 Peter 4:10 ESV

[35] Romans 8:38-39 ESV

[36] Isaiah 55:1-2 ESV

[37] 1 Corinthians 12:14 ESV

[38] John 3:5-6 ESV

[39] Colossians 3:3 NIV